My Dearest Cynthia,

It is clear to me why you are .... and passionate about what you believe. Your drive, motivation, and determination is all a part of your DNA. You are a part of such a rich history and heritage. The blood in your veins is from those who had so little yet sacrificed so much.

I am so proud that you are determined not to let such a great history die. By you putting the works of your great grandfather, Rev. Lewis Garnett Jordan, into print, his legacy and your legacy will now be propelled forward for the next generation. That is absolutely awesome!

What you have done in this work is not only tell the story of your loved one but you have told the story of the Black Baptist Church. You have invested so much, worked countless hours, and expressed immeasurable love to bring to life a wonderful history. Thank you for not allowing this part of our history to die. I am encouraged.

As your pastor I am so happy to call you a member of the Union Baptist Church of Hempstead, New York. I am also ever grateful that you have allowed me to be a part of your vision. It is my hope that you continue to share your gift with the world.

> Bountiful Blessings,
> Rev. Dr. Sedgwick V. Easley, Pastor
> Union Baptist Church
> Hempstead, New York

Lewis Garnett Jordan

The steps of a good man are ordered by the Lord.
                                        —*Psalm 37: 23*
*The greater the difficulty, the more the glory in sur-
mounting it.*

                                        —*Epicurus*

The African American journey can be summed up in words of the Negro National Anthem "Stony the road we Trod....." There is no story, no journey, and has been no struggle like that of our forefathers who faced oppression but yet were determined to overcome. They managed to use their limited resources to advance the Kingdom Agenda and give to the great cause of humanity.

This is evident with the life and legacy of Rev. Lewis G. Jordan. Although he was one generation removed from Africa, his insight and vision was far beyond his reality. He had values and ethics that can be seen through his works, his writings and his abiding faith. His scholarship and commitment to what he believed gave birth to much in the Black Baptist Church tradition.

The National Baptist Convention, especially the Foreign Mission Board, and the Baptist Church universal owe a debt of gratitude to Rev. Lewis G. Jordan and the countless other pioneers who sacrificed so much and yet had so little. His contributions, his scholarship, and his passion should never be forgotten.

                                        —Rev. Dr. Sedgwick V. Easley

March 15, 2016

Enjoy the Read!!

Cynthia H Cooper
Great Granddaughter of
Lewis G. Jordan

ON TWO HEMISPHERES

ON TWO HEMISPHERES

*Bits From The Life Story
Of Lewis G. Jordan*

As Told By Himself

with a Foreword by Cynthia D. Cooper

FCP

*Full Court Press
Englewood Cliffs, New Jersey*

Second Edition

First published in 1936
Foreword to the Second Edition
Copyright © 2013 by Cynthia D. Cooper

Published in the United States of America
by Full Court Press, 601 Palisade Avenue
Englewood Cliffs, NJ 07632
www.fullcourtpressnj.com

For further information about this book, write to:
Cynthia D. Cooper
P.O. Box 1208
Fort Lee, NJ 07024-9998

ISBN 978-1-938812-19-4
Library of Congress Control No. 2013947106

Editing and Book Design by Barry Sheinkopf for Bookshapers
(www.bookshapers.com)

Colophon by Liz Sedlack

1874 World Map courtesy istockphoto.com

Dedication

*To my daughter Robin, son Daniel,
and his future bride Jacqui*

Acknowledgments

For their generous help in the making of this book, I want to thank my cousins Darlene Butler-Davis and Chandler Sykes; Rev. Dr. Calvin O. Butts, and Rev. Nicholas S. Richards of the Abyssinian Baptist Church, Harlem, New York; Rev. Dr. Sedgwick V. Easley of the Union Baptist Church, Hempstead, New York; Rev. Herman Washington, Pastor of the Shiloh Baptist Church, Rockville Centre, New York; the Schomburg Center for Research in Black Culture, Harlem, New York; Larry and Olga Dais, Diane Whitfield, Lillian Dent, Wendy Ford, Debbie Lewis, Donald Coleman, Dr. Lisa Lehnert, Gloria Roberson, Dorothy Porter, Louise Chavous, and Gary and Sharon Griggs; Delores Kershaw and Gladys Andrew, my Sunday School teachers; Dr. and Mrs. Sedgwick V. Easley, Vanessa Pugh, Dorothy Smith, Ida Godwin, Leisa Dent and Stephanie Cooper, and Sister Easter Frye, my spiritual advisor. I also want to thank the tech staff at the New York Public Library at Forty-second Street, New York, for their help in scanning the original edition of this book, and to Barry Sheinkopf of Bookshapers for turning that scan of *On Two Hemispheres* into its second edition.

Introduction To The Second Edition

There is great truth and beauty in the life of Dr. Lewis Garnett Jordan, born a slave without a name but possessing a strong moral compass that pointed him home—home, that is. to Africa.

In his capacity as the third executive secretary of the Foreign Mission Board of Negro Baptist Churches, Jordan built hospitals and churches, and logged countless of miles as an ambassador of the faith.

Just twelve years before he assumed leadership of the Foreign Mission Board in 1896, colonial powers met in Berlin [1884–85] and decided the fate of the continent: It was to be divided up between European nations.

Famously, there were no Africans at the negotiating table; they were part of the parcel or scattered throughout the world, discounted as remnants with no agency.

But it did not take long for the remnants to return.

The hand that guided Mr. Jordan's evolution from slave to missionary is the very same that has seen the continent through the ravages of the last century and into the beginning of an economic renaissance brought about by the diligent work of countless descendants.

Among them stood Reverend Adam Clayton Powell, Sr., of the Abyssinian Baptist Church, who began to fashion the church into an instrument for social justice in America, a legacy that his son later continued.

Powell, Sr., who met Jordan and was inspired to support the Foreign Mission Board's work, also wrote the foreword for the first edition of Jordan's memoir *On Two*

Hemispheres.

Mr. Jordan aptly referred to the recollections in his memoir as *Bits*—remnants of a whole that contained the blueprint for self-determination for all the continent's descendants.

More than a century has passed since Jordan's pioneering work began.

As the ninth executive secretary of the Foreign Mission Board, I live and breathe his work wherever I go, from the library he built in Malawi to the people who still remember him in Liberia.

As I compose the words to accompany the re-release of Jordan's memoir, gratitude fills me for the man who forged the path before me. And I remain more determined than ever to strive for a Free Africa, an Africa that decides its own destiny. This is the Africa Dr. Jordan and I dream of. This is the Africa we will create.

—*The Rev. Nicholas S. Richards*
Executive Secretary
Foreign Mission Board
National Baptist Convention USA, Inc.

Foreword to the Second Edition

Ethiopia shall soon stretch out
Her Hands unto God.
—Psalm 68: 31

Pharaoh King of Egypt issued a decree freeing the slaves of Egypt. Did he see it as an idea whose time had come? How, similarly, can a proclamation written by Abraham Lincoln, over one hundred and fifty years ago, free millions of Africans with the swipe of a quill pen? Did he wake up one morning and realize the time was right for the emancipation of Africans? Were the slaves emancipated, or were the shackles that bound our country broken and democracy freed to flourish? I pondered these questions as I held the book written by my great-grandfather, Lewis Garnett Jordan (1853–1939), a former slave, active in the early years of the Philadelphia Baptist Convention and Corresponding Secretary of the Foreign Mission Board of the National Baptist Convention from 1896 to 1922. What was going through the mind of this 10-year-old child born into slavery? Where did the light come from that illuminated his mind? Did he see the world any differently after the shackles of slavery were broken? What did freedom feel like for him—and so many others?

And it shall be for a sign and for
a witness unto the Lord of hosts in
the land of Egypt: for thy shall cry
unto the Lord because of the
oppressors, and he shall send them a
savior, and a great one, and he shall
deliver them.
—Isaiah 19:20

Sitting patiently on a shelf, in the rare books department of the Schomburg Center For Research in Black Culture, as if waiting for me, was great-grandfather Jordan's work. With trembling hands I first held the book, *On Two Hemispheres, Bits from the Life Story of Lewis G. Jordan*. I felt so much love for him; I became hypnotized by his words, his passion became my passion, his fear became my fear, his sadness brought tears to my eyes, and his courage to move forward gave me courage to never give up on my dreams. He has imprinted his soul into mine. "Lo, I will be with you always even to the end of time."

And so, with deep abiding faith, constant prayer and a humbling spirit, I decided it was time to again share his story with you.

—*Cynthia D. Cooper*

Aunt Addie's Letter

Some of the best conversation starts around the dinner table, and that evening was no different.

Robin and Aunt Addie were chatting away. Robin began asking Addie about family history, and to her delight she shared a story with Robin about her great-great-grandfather. As the evening drew to a close and we were about to leave, Aunt Addie promised to write Robin a note documenting our family history.

Here is the letter she wrote:

December 18 1979

Dear Robin,
    — I promised you a note in
reference to your great great grandfather.
His name was Lewis G. Jordan DD.
He was a pastor of the Union Baptist
Church Phila, Pa.
    In 1896 he became the Corresponding
Secretary of the Foreign Mission Board
of Negro Baptist Churches U.S.A. He served
for 26 years and retired in 1921
He was an authority on Foreign Mission
information.
    He made 4 trips across the seas
to Africa and the West Indies and
6 trips to Europe in the interest
of the Foreign Mission Board.
He was honored as Corresponding
Secretary Emeritus which title he
held until after his death Feb. 25, 1939
His works will be found in the
Schomburg Collection & Library located
    110 - 135th Street New York City, N.Y.

over

He is the Author of
1. Pebbles from an African Beach
2. Negro Baptist History
3 Church Directory & Busy Pastors Guide
4 On Two Hemispheres (Bits from
   the life story of Lewis G. Jordan)

Have a very Merry Xmas.
Visit us when you can.
We will be pleased to see
you.

                With love
                Aunt Addie

   P.S.
Lewis Garnett Jordans grandchildren are:
1. Cynthia Sykes Butler
2 Emma Sykes Harrison (deceased)
3. Adelaide Sykes Langley
4 Chandler Whitmore Sykes
5 Elleary Davis Williams Smith

The George Lisle Monument, of Italian marble, in the front yard of the
First Bryant Baptist Church, Savannah, Georgia. In loving memory of Amer-
ican Baptists' first Foreign Missionary. It was erected in 1916, by the National
Baptist Convention, U.S.A., through its Foreign Mission Board.

Rev. A.R. Robinson, D.D., Chairman
Rev. J.R. Bennett, D.D., Recording Secretary
Rev. W.F. Graham, D.D., Treasurer
L. G. Jordan, D.D., Corresponding Secretary

Preface to the First Edition

"Stir me, Oh stir me Lord, I care not how,
But stir my heart with passion for the world.
Stir me to go,-to give,-but most to pray;
Stir till the blood-red banner be unfurled
O'er lands that still in deepest darkness lie,
O'er deserts where no cross is lifted high.

Stir me, stir even me. Thyself wast stirred,
By love's intensest fire, till Thou didst give
Thine only Son, Thy best beloved One,
E'en to the cruel cross that I might live.
Stir me to give myself so back to Thee,
That Thou canst give Thyself again through me."

For more than a decade my friends have urged me to write a little story of my life, till now at last I myself have the urge-so here it is. If any kind reader regards this booklet as a jumbled affair, he must remember it is only bits and not in the least intended to be a connected narrative. If in this whole booklet there chances to be a single thought-provoking *Bit*, I praise God for it, hoping it will help someone and be passed on.

—L.G.J.

Introduction To The First Edition

Someone has said that a book which is not worth the second reading is not worth reading at all. With intense interest I have read *Bits* twice. In many respects it is the most unique autobiography I have seen.

It is an informing review of the closing days of American slavery and the fierce struggle of the years which followed the Emancipation Proclamation, when the ex-slaves fought heroically to make a place for the Negro in the sun.

Among those early pioneers the name of Dr. L.G. Jordan will ever be near the top of the list. His life, work, and service is nothing less than a miracle. Here is a man who came out of slavery without a name. He borrowed a name from three different men, and his career has been an honor to each of them. Not having a birthday, he selected one for himself and never felt a pair of trousers rub his legs until he had possibly passed his tenth year.

Out of those borrowed trousers came one of the best preachers and church builders the race has produced, and a temperance advocate who won the respect of the American people, who gave him a nomination for the United States Congress on the Prohibition ticket. Out of those old baggy trousers emerged the secretary of the National Baptist Foreign Mission Board, who served in that capacity unstintingly and sacrificially for twenty-five years, and who today is the best informed colored missionary in the world. Fifty years hence, when our petty jealousies have disappeared, some unprejudiced historian will give him first place among Negroes in world-wide kingdom building.

I first met the author of *Bits* in 1892. He was then pastor of the Union Baptist Church, Philadelphia. He gave me my first vision of Foreign Missions at a meeting at his church, which was addressed by himself and Dr. Luke.

From that day until now, every church of which I have been pastor has supported Foreign Missions. For fifteen years the Abyssinian Church has paid the salary of a missionary in Africa. We are now supporting two missionaries in Liberia. The credit is due Dr. Jordan. Hundreds of Baptist ministers could tell the same story if they would. They will, after Jordan falls on sleep. Negroes are like alcohol—they kill the living, and preserve the dead.

Gratefully yours,
A. Clayton Powell, Sr.
New York, New York

In His service, I am
L.G. Jordan

MISS LUCY W. SMITH
Kentucky
Historian—American National
Baptist Convention

REV. W.W. COLLEY, D.D.
Foremost in the organization of the National Baptist Convention; first Corresponding Secretary and first missionary to African fields of that body. Born in Prince Edward County, VA, February 12, 1847. Died in Winston-Salem, NC, December 24, 1909.

REV. W.H. MCALPINE, D.D.
First President of the National Baptist Convention. He served two terms and refused a third election. Founder and second President of Selma University and Editor of the Baptist Pioneer, a state paper. Born in Buckingham County, VA, June 1847; died in Selma, AL, 1905.

REV. J.M. ARMISTEAD, D.D.
First Recording Secretary of the National Baptist Convention; Pastor of Zion Baptist Church, Portsmouth, VA, for over 45 years. Though among our older men, he was still active and much beloved by his people. He is one of only 8 out of 151 original delegates of the Convention still alive.

RUFUS L. PERRY, Ph.D.
New York
Historian—American Baptist
Missionary Convention

WILLIAM TROY, D.D.
Virginia
Historian—Consolidated
Missionary Baptist Convention

RICHARD D. BAPTISTE, D.D.
Illinois
Historian—National
Baptist Convention

ALLEN R. GRIGGS, D.D.
Texas
Historian—Baptist Foreign
Missionary Convention of
North America

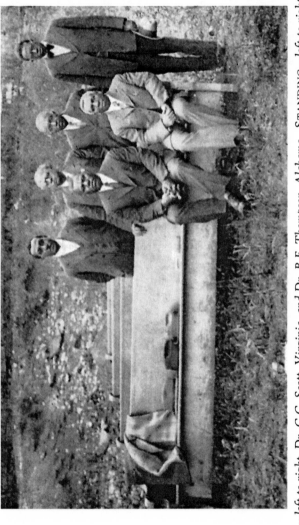

SEATED—left to right, Dr. C.C. Scott, Virginia, and Dr. B.F. Thompson, Alabama. STANDING—left to right, Dr. Spurgeon Davis, Alabama; L.G. Jordan, Tennessee; Dr. W.H. Jernagin, Washington, DC; and Dr. J.P Barbour. About three years before this photograph was taken, during the Foreign Mission Conference in Montgomery, AL I secured the help of these brethren to carry the pews shown here from the basement of the First Baptist Church into the yard. The pews are those that were used in 1880 by the men and women at the organizing of the Foreign Mission Convention, U.S.A., the progenitor of the National Baptist Convention.

CHAPTER 1

WAS BORN ON A farm in Lauderdale County,
Mississippi, about halfway between Enterprise
and Meridian. I have no way of knowing the
day of my birth. My mother was what was called a
"Guinea Negro." Her father had been brought to Alabama
from the Guinea Coast of Africa when about eighteen
years of age. He was drowned in the Mississippi River
somewhere near Delta, Louisiana, in a desperate effort to
escape from Louisiana back to Alabama, where he had
been sold away from three small children (Mariah,
Tenah, and Levi), whose mother was dead. So I often say
I am only one generation removed from Africa.

My Mother
and Earliest Childhood Recollections

"Long may our land be bright,
With Freedom's holy light;
Protect us by thy might;
Great God our King!"

My mother told me that when I was just a tiny little fellow, crawling about in some new ground that had been cleared up where we lived in Mississippi, having recently moved from Alabama, I found a rattlesnake under the house. She heard me laughing in first one place then another, and soon I set up a distressing wail, as anyone of my size would have done in such a situation. It afterwards appeared I had been following the snake around and at last had attempted to pick it up, whereupon it bit me on the wrist in its anger; I crawled out on one side of the house and the snake on the other where, making for the bushes, it was killed by my mother. Buried in "indigo mud" and drenched with "cocklebur tea," so I was told, my life was saved; but the same bite-scar I still have. Sometime later, on a Saturday afternoon, my mother, after a hard week's work, was washing for the "white folks," and I climbed on a bench to a tub of clothes ready for hanging up and put my little dirty hands on them. The mistress was passing at the time and in a rage slapped me from the bench, several feet away. Mother, like an enraged lioness, collared her mistress and nearly choked her to death. Of course she was severely flogged by the master for it, but it took nearly the remaining afternoon to do so. From that time until freedom came, the master never attempted to whip her without a gun near at hand and being sure that she was well tied.

The sight of her bleeding back and her mournful cries for mercy and pity as the blows from a cowhide rained on her bare back will always remain in my memory.

My father, it seemed, was a shiftless or wandering young Spaniard by the name of Jack Gaddis, whose brother, Neal Gaddis, was a planter and slaveholder not far away. There are several reasons why I have never taken my father's name. In the first place, I did not know of this before I was nearly a man. Second, he was known as a "white man," and I as a Negro, and I know he would not own me, and so I did not own him. I was a slave of a "poor white man," David Nutt, who owned only my mother with her three children and her sister, who had one child. He owned us through marriage. My master was drafted as a Confederate soldier, it seems, but his brother-in-law, Will Carey, went as a substitute for him, leaving him to care for the farm and a large family. This brother-in-law was wounded (in what battle I do not know), but he was brought back home, and during the long days gradually grew worse. It was my duty to ward off the flies and mosquitoes with a brush pulled from a chinaberry tree (screens were unknown in those days). I remember when he finally died, forgetting my relief from the long vigil, the battle with the insects, and how often I had been slapped over for nodding and letting the bush annoy the sick man, when I could not help it, I wept in my childish way and mourned with the family. Then my master was compelled to go to war himself. He took me with him to Enterprise, where I gathered firewood, washed pots and pans, and performed other little tasks for his "mess" or squad. I do not know how long I was kept in this Confederate camp.

Misunderstanding with a Mule

I do not know how old I was when sent to the "old Dunn" mill, on the Chunkey River, to have corn ground into meal for bread and the bran for coffee. Part of the time, during the Civil War, we were so blockaded and hemmed in, the outer world could not ship to us coffee; hence, okra seed meal bran was toasted and used instead for coffee. I am sure it was in war-times. My owner owned only one large horse, Jake, and one small mule, Jack; mother plowed Jake and they sent me to the mill on Jack. As a boy I saw every kind of squirrel as Jack slowly walked along, shying now and again as a stump, root, or other objects were approached, and often he pitched me over his head as he dodged. Climbing a long hill, the corn began rolling back, and, Jack being short, I soon found myself and the corn on the ground, having slipped off over the rear end of Jack.

What did he do? He walked to the roadside and began eating grass; when I tried to catch him, he backed his ears, switched his tail, keeping his heel trained on me, and continued to eat, so I could not get hold of the bridle. I coaxed and cried, but Jack wouldn't give in. I then got a brush, Jack trotted off, and I followed him home. Mother had to stop plowing, catch Jack, and, going to where the corn lay, put it on Jack again and started me on to the mill afresh. This occurred in one way or the other many times, and they finally let me ride Jake because he was sway-backed and I could not slip off.

As the war drew to a close the slaves were shifted here and yonder, and we were carried to the canebrakes, and in a remote spot, perhaps as large as an average-sized house, cleared of cane, were hidden so as not to fall into the hands of the Yankees, who were pictured to us as dreadful ogres to be shunned at all hazards, and I firmly believed it all. One day while the master was seated on the porch, he saw some Yankees coming; grabbing his gun, he ran for tall timber, and I ran with him, but the Yankees on horses and with clicking guns ran him down and ordered, "Halt!" and he halted. Then I squatted in the weeds while they carried him back to the house—terrified, I ran further on into the woods.

REV. NATHANIEL H. PIUS, A.B., D.D.

Of all our men and women who undertook gathering historical data about Negro Baptists, that collected by Dr. Pius alone was printed in book form. He issued the 154-page Outline of Baptist History *in 1911.*

As victors, men with whom I worked and our comrades in the Lord,
they have achieved and now rest under the shade of the tree of life.

Wesley F. Graham, D.D.—Born 1858, in Mississippi; reared in Arkansas; educated in Wayland Seminary; pastored in Virginia and Pennsylvania; died in Philadelphia, 1932. A great preacher and treasurer of the National Baptist Convention.

Edward W. Isaac, D.D.—Born 1863, in Louisiana; reared in Texas; educated in Bishop College; Eloquent preacher, dynamic debater, organizer, and secretary of the B.Y.P.U. Board; died May 30, 1931, in Nashville, TN.

Robert B. Hudson, A.M.—Born and reared in Alabama; an educator of high rank; outstanding layman and financier; Secretary of the National Baptist Convention. Died in Selma, AL.

Emanuel M. Lawrence, D.D.—Born June 1, 1861, and reared in Tennessee. Educated in Roger Williams University and served as trustee and treasurer of that school. Died October 9, 1929, in Nashville, TN.

J. Francis Robinson, D.D.—Gifted preacher and field secretary of the Sunday School Publishing Board. Died in Chicago.

Peter James Bryant, D.D.—Born and reared in Georgia; was a protege of Drs. E.K. Love, Lyons, and Walker. An excellent pastor, forceful debater, and wise leader. Died in Atlanta.

S.B. Butler, D.D.—Striking in personality, though quiet and unassuming; was preacher of power. Treasurer of S.S. and B.Y.P.U. Congress. Died in Indianapolis, IN.

Adam Daniel Williams, D.D.—Born January 1863. A Georgian by birth; was educated at Morehouse and ranked as Baptist leader in his state and the nation. Treasurer of the National Baptist Convention. Died March 1931.

William M. Taylor, D.D.—Born and reared in Louisiana; educated in Leland University. Prominent in leadership and a relentless opponent. A convincing preacher and a fatherly pastor. Vice-president-at-large of the National Baptist Convention. Died in Baton Rouge, LA.

Charles Roberson, Attorney at Law—Native of Louisiana. Successful lawyer and staunch Baptist layman. Visited Europe and Africa. Was attorney for the National Baptist Convention during its most stormy period. Died in his hometown, Shreveport, LA.

Edward D. Pierson, Auditor—Master printer, successful teacher, recognized public accountant; served as Efficiency Director of the National Baptist Convention; died in Indiana, April 14, 1930.

12. Charles H. Parrish, A. M., D. D.—A Fellow of the Royal Geographical Society, England. A lover of his native state, Kentucky. Educated in Simmons University and later elected to its presidency. Served as chairman of the Foreign Mission Board and visited Europe and the West Indies in the interest of that work. A good pastor, wise counselor and persistent contender of the cause in which he believed. He served as statistician for the National Baptist Convention. Died in Louisville, KY.

13. Edward P. Johnson, D. D.—One of the best and most pious leaders of his day. Pastor and teacher. Educated at Morehouse College, he later became Dean of its Theological Department. An excellent pastor with an unusual love for missions. Died in Atlanta, age 81.

14. W.W. Brown, D.D.—Native of Virginia. God led him in a marvelous way to enrich, enlarge, and cultivate many churches. As an evangelistic pastor, he had few equals; he gripped his hearers with fingers of steel, and no man among us surpassed him as a man of prayer. When he awakened to Africa's needs—while pastoring in Roanoke, VA, he became an ardent advocate for the missionary cause and later sowed seeds in the hearts of hundreds in Pittsburgh and New York while pastoring in those cities. His was the first church to give $1,000 per year to missions, and later they took upon themselves the entire support of a missionary in Africa at $1,500 per year. He died in New York City.

15. Charles Satchell Morris, D. D.—Born September 1865 in Louisville, KY, he was educated in Howard University, D.C., and Newton Center, MA. He was a dependable friend, and was uncommonly brotherly in his relations with his fellow men. He visited more sections of the Black Continent than anyone among us except the present writer, and his eloquence won the interest and helpfulness of many. He combined good business qualities with power as a preacher and great patience and lovableness as a pastor. He fell asleep in Jesus in July 1931 at Richmond, VA.

CHAPTER 2

"The history of the Negro, whether national or domestic, is written in blood. . .violently wrested from his home and condemned to toil without hope by Christians to whom be had done no wrong."
—From "An Appeal in Favor of that Class of Americans Called Africans," 1836

 E WERE RETAINED AS slaves quite a while longer than necessary because, panic-stricken, I ran away from the dreaded Yankees when they passed our place, taking our horse and mule. And since Mother did not know just where I was nor what might befall me if my faithful mother went on with the others and left me behind, she refused to leave.

When I returned to the cabin, I found her grieving over the loss of her opportunity to leave under protection of the Yankees, who, she explained to me, were our friends, and if we had gone with them it would have meant I would wear pants and shoes like the young master. Her tender words finally calmed my fears, and I became as anxious as she to get away.

But the master watched the cabins so closely for the next few days, there was no chance to escape his vigilance. Living far from the main road, most of the Union soldiers had been mustered out of service before a second chance came for women and children to escape. Finally we got word that two regiments of soldiers, one white, the other black, were still stationed in Meridian. A slave man who had been to the Yankee camps came to our cabin late one night and helped my mother and her sister arrange for the adventure of find-ing freedom. It was planned that I was to wait until the mistress was asleep and then get her shoes for my mother to "wear to freedom." I do not recall that she took anything else with her as part recompense for the long years of toil, but I waited around after I had put the little white children to bed, and when I was sure the master and mistress were sound asleep, I got the shoes, so my mother would have them to "wear to free-dom."

On a dark night in a downpour of rain, we set out, wading creeks and lagoons in our flight. Only a kind Providence saved us from drowning. Although our journey to the city would not ordinarily have been over twelve miles in extent, yet to evade the bloodhounds we could hear baying in the distance we covered twice as many miles. (I have traveled over this route several times since and have learned this fact.)

However, we arrived at daylight and were happy beyond description in finding the much-coveted free-dom under the protection of humane, kind-hearted sol-diers.

> *"I have had many things in my hands, and I have lost them all, but whatever I have been able to place in God's hands I still possess."*
>
> —*Martin Luther*

I recall that one of the soldiers, whom they called "Lewis"—I do not recall his surname—was especially good to me and gave me the first pair of trousers I had ever worn; they of course were too long and very baggy on me, but I managed to wear them by methods of my own invention.

Up to this time I had no name. I had never been called anything but "Nig," short for Nigger. The need for a name developed when, soon after we entered the camp, a good lady from Newark, Ohio, opened a school for the "contraband chillun," as we were called, in an empty barrack. As I recall, her name was Miss Mary E. Reeves; gathering these small all ex-slaves around her in the improvised schoolroom, Miss Reeves explained to us that she must enroll each child's name; I remember how they told her their names: Mary, John, Adam, Eff, and so on, and when she finally came to me, I hated to tell her my name was "Nigger"; in my dilemma, I remembered the soldier who gave me the pants, and I gave "Lewis" as my name.

But my problem was not fully solved. "Lewis what?" she asked. My little mind, like a rose-bud grown in the shade, worked slowly, but I finally remembered that another soldier whose name was Jordan had given me a blouse, so I appropriated his name also, and was put down on the list as Lewis Jordan. Next day she told us that she was going to call the roll and each child must answer, "Present." When she called, "Lewis Jordan," no one responded, for I had entirely forgotten I had named myself, and when all the children looked around for the boy, I looked around, too.

But the thoughtful teacher remembered me and, looking me straight in the eye, said, "Isn't your name Lewis Jordan?"

Like a flash I answered, "Present," and after a few

days' drilling I took it for granted that my name was Lewis Jordan and not "Nigger."

Strange as it may seem, in drifting around, by some means my name has been changed several times—Lewis Griffin and Lewis King—but the Jordan stuck with me. Years later, when I had learned to read, I chanced on "The Rising Sun" by William Wells Brown, which contained the account of a Presbyterian minister Rev. Henry Highland Garnett; I had learned by then that many people had three names, and I liked the name Garnett very much, so I promptly annexed that also, putting it between the other two, and hence throughout the years have been known as Lewis Garnett Jordan.

Our teacher at the beginning spent quite a little time teaching us the words "Jesus loves me, this I know, for the Bible tells me so," and "Sweet hour of prayer that calls me from this world of care." Such words I had never heard before; oh! the effect on my child heart can never be described. Then she followed with: "Our Father who art in heaven, Hallowed be thy name."

Some Easy Things to Do

> "Make a mistake. To be mistaken. Get angry too quick. Act hastily. Judge others."
>
> —Selected

One of the reasons I have tried to give any person under accusation the benefit of the doubt arises in a gruesome experience I had while still a small chap. We had safely dodged the bloodhounds and escaped to the protection of Union soldiers near Meridian. I was making myself as useful as an urchin of my age could, helping one of the soldiers in a white regiment, receiving hard tack and navy beans as pay. One morning following "pay day," my benefactor found that the wallet containing all his money was missing from its place of hiding in his tent. After a thorough search and questioning his comrades, they seemed to agree unanimously that no one but this little Negro had taken it. (Just from bondage, I had seen only a few 5-, 10-, and 25-cent pieces, and as now I remember, I would not have picked up a green back bill had I seen it on the road, not knowing its value.)

They began to threaten me with hanging if I did not tell the truth and return the wallet. In vain I protested and declared my innocence. I was to meet with a speedy death if I did not confess. So at last in desperation and to end the torture—as I thought—I "confessed." Of course this only sunk me further in the mire of my trouble, for now more misery followed their question: "Where is it?"

Naturally, I felt that relief from this dreadful nightmare would come if I could get to Mother, and I sobbed out that it was "Home." Little knowing what this would mean to my mother, I sought the shortest cut to the wretched cabin with its dirt floor in the "corral," which was the only home I knew, the search party following.

My mother, as innocent as a newborn babe of the theft, was frightened nearly out of her wits by the crowd, the noisy threats, and my danger. The searching was soon over, and off they trotted me to the woods to make good their promise to hang me "by the neck till I was dead."

With the thought that I was seeing my mother's face for the last time, I was taken to the forest. It must have been that they were convinced I was not guilty by this time, for, exhausted by the ordeal I had passed through, I cried myself to sleep while they sat around and I awaited execution.

When I awoke, it was possibly four in the afternoon and I was alone; the soldiers had returned to their camps, and I was about two miles from home, but the psychological effect of their accusation has remained in my memory to this day. Thoroughly convinced of my innocence, I presume, two days later I was back at my old job carrying water and doing other little chores. I was too small to ask and too ignorant to really care whether they ever discovered the culprit and got back the wallet and the money or not. I was too happy at being allowed to live and to be busy at my tasks. Then as now, there was little or no redress for a Negro when falsely accused and arrested.

CHAPTER 3

Kidnapped

*"Fleecy locks and dark complexion
Cannot forfeit Nature's claim;
Skins may differ, but Affection
Dwells in white and black the same."*
—Cowper

 HE PRESENT EPIDEMIC OF kidnapping re-
minds me of a great sorrow: About 1866,
when my Aunt Tenah was kidnapped by a
former slaveholder some months after our escape to
freedom, and we never heard of her again. Melvina, my
older sister, who was about seven years old, was also
carried off about the same time. Corporal Dorsey, of
the 48th U. S. Colored Infantry, had asked Mother to
let her go to Vicksburg as nurse for his baby, and on
refusal, as the children gathered by the music of the
regiment band, he knew her and carried her off. I was

in another car, on the same train, and only saw her at the end of our journey. I saw her twice as she sat in the sun, on a winter day, bare-footed, nursing Corporal Dorsey's babe on Ft. Hill, Vicksburg. Ignorant as I was, how I longed to get word to my mother or in some way get sister back, but I was helpless and soon passed on to Natchez, Mississippi, my new home. Later I learned she afterwards went to live with a Rev. Smothers but never learned how she got away from Corporal Dorsey, nor have I ever seen or heard of her since. Those were slavery days. Thank God they will never come again.

I went to live with a man by the name of Peter Griffin, who was an orderly sergeant in the 52nd Colored Regiment, in Natchez. My mother was grief-stricken over her losses; she knew where I was, it is true, but that to her was as far a distance as if it were in the moon. This man called himself "adopting" me, so she was bereft of us all. The family of Mr. Griffin, my adopted father, was in Ohio, but after being mustered out of the army he lived at Natchez, in Folies Alley, with his sister, Mrs. Agnes Robinson, and here he placed me to live. She was a devout member of the A. M. E. church, and now for the first time in my life I was situated so that I could attend Sunday school and day school regularly. To the best of my knowledge I must have been there more than two years, and during that time they saw to it that I went to school, for which I bless their memories. Mrs. Robinson had me christened as Lewis Griffin in the A. M. E. church, by Dr.

Clark.

After school hours and on Saturdays, I sold home-made pies at the boat-landing (for those were days of great steamboats and few railroads in our country) and elsewhere for "Aunt Agnes," as I called her. Often, wicked men and larger boys would steal or take my pies from me, and not pay for them; then my auntie would report the losses to my adopted father, and in every case no excuse was taken, but I was severely flogged. I often told my troubles to my teachers, who were sympathetic Yankee folk, and at last they gave me money enough to buy a ticket to Vicksburg. To the best of my knowledge I was under twelve years old at that time. After leaving Natchez, I finally secured work on a steamboat that was in part or wholly owned by a colored man, Thomas W. Stringer, who later founded and became a great man in the K. of P. and Masons. The boat was a side-wheeler—"The Countess," and traded in the "Bends."

In time I wandered back to Meridian, walking most of the 140 miles to see my mother and to escape Mr. Griffin. While out there, I worked for a Mr. Alfred King on a rich man's farm near where I was born; working for my "victuals and clothes" which were both very poor. In preparing this account I find myself recording time by Christmas or cotton picking time, and it is not accurate only as to incidents.

After possibly two years of this hard life, I went back to Vicksburg and steamboated until I went to live on a farm with a Mr. William Shannon on Belks Island near Davis Bend and later on from which place I drifted into the meeting where I was converted—saved!

The island was across "Ole Mississippi" River, on which the revival was being conducted by a Rev. Leven Wood. Hearing of the large number who were "getting religion," all that was within me craved to find that new way. In his sermons the preacher stressed 1 John 5:1: "He that believeth that Jesus is the Christ is born of God." I believed made an open confession of my Lord, and was born of God. I became converted along with eighty others, among them Hon. Isa. T. Montgomery and Benj. T. Green; these men were founders of Mound Bayou.

We were all baptized in August on the Jeff Davis plantation in the Mississippi River in Warren County. In the meantime, my mother, whom I had not seen for possibly two or more years, secured a position as cook for a Southern Methodist preacher. When he left, he recommended her to the next minister, and so for twelve or more years she served in this way, and then married a man by the name of Benjamin Phillips from Livingston, Alabama. Because of their poor way of managing their affairs, they both became my charges. He died first, and my mother lived with or near me nearly forty years until her death in Philadelphia, Pennsylvania in 1922, at the age of about ninety years. When about sixteen or seventeen years of age (according to a birthday I had by this time fixed for myself), I was working on a farm in Davis Bend. A good man, Gus Williams, who thought I could preach, took me to

Dr. Emery in Vicksburg and asked that he have me preach. The good doctor sized me up and said bluntly, "I would not have that boy in my pulpit." After I was grown and had become a pastor in San Antonio, Texas, where Dr. Emery, afterwards Bishop Emery, was pastoring also, I was called upon to preach his wife's funeral, and did so without thought of the past or any resentment.

On September 12, 1873, I was licensed to preach in the Bend. I was ordained November 1874 at Cottonwood near Lake Providence, Louisiana, and entered the pastorate of my first church—Yazoo City, Mississippi, in 1875. Feeling keenly the need of more preparation, I entered the Bible Institute in 1879 (afterwards Roger Williams University), Nashville, Tennessee. Dr. D. W. Phillips was president and Dr. L. B. Tefft dean.

On Christmas Day in 1879, I baptized a large number in Tchular Lake for the Bethlehem Church, to which I gave one Sunday a month as pastor. That night I went through the country more than 25 miles to take the train for Nashville, Tennessee, to go to school. On getting ready for school, I persuaded the parents or six young people out of my churches to send them with me.

So Jacob Bennett, Oliver Taylor, Albert Stevens, Emma Rundles, Sallie Doty, and Mary Turner all went to school with me, as their pastor. What I had learned years before, as baker on steamboats, came in good, as I became baker for the school to help meet my bills and assist Taylor and Bennett. The real spirit of gratitude shown by Rev. J. R. Bennett for the kindness was the purest I ever knew.

All of these young people have given a good account of themselves—one a doctor and great church worker in the District of Columbia, one a pastor, and all three girls good teachers, wives, and mothers.

CHAPTER IV

An Early Help That Lasted

Ignorance of prayer is a great misfortune, but prayerlessness is death. To master its secrets there must be uncompromising surrender, the unhesitating uncovering of our hearts to the scrutiny of Christ. This surrender is both an act and an attitude.
—William E. Doughty

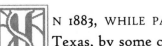N 1883, WHILE PASTORING in San Antonio, Texas, by some chance I got hold of *Lectures to Students* by Charles H. Spurgeon.

I had not read far until it seemed I was face to face with questions like the following with answers demanded:

Why am I preaching? Is it because I am lazy, because it is a good place to show off, or am I called of God and know I am preaching because first, I want to obey him, second, because I love the soul and body of men and wish to see them do well in this world and eventually saved in heaven? The lectures awakened anew all I ever heard about preaching. I was startled, I was humbled.

When I came to "The Preacher's Private Prayer" chapter and read the following: "Of course the preacher is above all others distinguished as a man of prayer. He prays as an ordinary Christian, else he were a hypocrite. He prays more than ordinary Christians, else he were disqualified for the office which he has undertaken."

I wept bitterly and prayed to be more humble, more earnest, more unselfish, and more useful. I had been pastoring then for only ten years but for these other fifty-two years Mr. Spurgeon's *Lectures to Students* has influenced my whole life, increased my respect and love for ideals, made me rely on God in prayer, and made me to more loyally serve my denomination and my God.

For forty years I have reported annually to the National Convention, and in nearly every report I have urged my brethren that we deepen our prayer lives by enlarging our prayer lives if we would have our ministry a greater success and our whole dispositions sweetened.

Madam Sisiretta Jones told me, "As a concert singer I never go before the footlights until I have knelt in my dressing room and prayed." So I have urged all who sing or work in his name to pray that the song or message may be blessed with point and winged with power.

Thus Far the Lord Hath Led Me On

> *"I would rather train one man to pray than ten*
> *men to preach. Such pastors cannot fail to make their*
> *congregations grapple with the realities of the king-*
> *dom.*
> —George H. C. McGregor

As I look in retrospect over the vista of the past, I am reminded what General Armstrong, the wise and good, the great founder of Hampton Institute often said when questioned concerning the beginning of his work and the source of his ideas about: "I did not consciously set out to do any special thing and it seemed that I was led without my own effort from one step to another." In much the same way I had been prepared for my own ventures in life.

For instance, my hatred for liquor and its effects on the minds and bodies of men began when I learned in very early childhood to shun my master, usually kind and generous, but transformed into a wild, cursing, howling demon when be was drunk. I still bear scars that were left from the beating which nearly cost my little life when, accompanied by a jug of whiskey, he came home one day yelling like a Comanche Indian and caught a glimpse of me running to find shelter in the hiding place his wife and children always sought when he was having one of his "spells." I could not have been more than five or six years old. Years later, when I had gone to Texas, and was pastor of New Hope Baptist Church, the state decided to vote on an amendment to its constitution prohibiting the sale of intoxicating liquors for beverage purposes; it seemed only natural that, as a preacher in the community, I should do all I could to crystallize sentiment in favor of the amendment. A saloon-keeper and owner of a hotel informed one of my deacons that I was meddling with things that "were none of my business," and the deacon, a leading hack driver, with a stand at this hotel, after getting others to join him, called on me to show me the error of my ways and to point out what it would mean in injury to the church if I continue to talk against "their personal liberty" to drink the "red liquor."

Thereupon I informed him, because of the injury the liquor was doing to my people, that I would always fight the traffic and would at once, rather than injure the church, sever my connection with it. I shall always recall using the following expression: "I have my time and a little talent to dispose of, but my convictions are my own and not for sale."

I resigned at prayer-meeting Friday night, to take effect Sunday night. Within less than a week, with a wife and two children, I was without a church and with no prospect of work in sight. But it appeared that my arguments for prohibition had attracted the attention of Dr. B. H. Carroll, revered and loved by Southern Baptists, who was then pastoring to Waco and later on became President of the Theological Seminary in Fort Worth. Dr. Carroll was also Chairman of the State Prohibition Committee and lost no time in sending for me to inquire about the whole matter, and forthwith I was sent out to fight as a "stump speaker" for the amendment. When the liquor element finally won out, I went with recommendations from Dr. Carroll and others as a delegate to the National Prohibition Convention, which held its meeting in Chicago that year (1888). I was among the delegates to the Prohibition Convention, which nominated General Clinton B. Fisk for president, and Dr. John A. Brooks for vice-president. Subsequently I canvassed the states of Illinois, Nebraska, Iowa, and South Dakota in the interest of the Prohibition Party.

I was fortunate in gaining the friendship and interest of many men and women whose names were household words in temperance annals: Gen. Clinton B. Fisk, Miss Frances E. Willard, Gov. Jno. P. St. John, Mrs. Helen M. Gouger, and others. I spoke at rallies with them all.

CHAPTER V

My First Trip to Africa

"There are pioneer souls that blaze their paths
Where highways never ran
But let me live by the side of the road
And be a friend to man."

—Sam Walter Foss

N 1883 I MOVED from Mississippi into Texas, and at different times pastored Second Baptist Church in San Antonio; New Hope in Waco; First Church in Anderson; and St. Immanuel at Hearne, Texas. At each of these places I planned and led in building some of the best churches of that day.

In 1885, while I was pastor of New Hope Church, Waco, a number of my parishioners somehow became members of an organization which was planning to form a colony of emigrants to West Africa. Restive and dissatisfied with what they regarded as oppression in this country, they longed for a land where they might have self-determination and have a part in shaping the affairs and the laws under which they would live.

Being a busy preacher, I was at first indifferent, but as one after another of my members drifted to the movement, my interest in the undertaking gradually grew. At last they seemed to have found it advisable to send someone as an advance courier to report on the country to which they were preparing to emigrate rather than to leave as a body for an unknown territory.

Someone, they decided, should go to Africa and bring back information about the character of the soil, what it would produce, the principal foods grown there; 'to see if they could secure land; to learn whether the staple food plants of America would thrive in that climate; to find out what equipment was best to take with them, and in short to understand more about conditions there. To my surprise a committee waited on me to ask if I would go and bring back to them this information. After some little hesitation, I finally consented and just 12 days later, in February, 1885, I was on my way to Africa, not half equipped for such a trip. None of us had the intelligence to think much of money for my return trip. Of course they promised to send me money. My trip took me through Liverpool, England, the Madeiras, Cape Verde Islands, and thence to Cape Mount after a journey of nearly five weeks.

My Report

On my return I reported to my people that cotton, corn, and all of our vegetables would grow in Liberia; many grew perpetually because there was no frost, but there was no one to furnish subsistence supplies, the peck of meal, 4 lbs. of meal and the pint of molasses which we are accustomed to when working on farms in this country; no spray for the insects, which were far more numerous and deadly than we have here in this country. Those who went, I explained, would be pioneers and might have to do as the Pilgrims who landed at Plymouth Rock and Jamestown—eat parched corn and roots. The result was that only a few, if any, went at that time. On my visit I met Dr. and Mrs. W. W. Colley, Rev. J. H. Presley, and three of our six workers at Grand Cape Mount, Liberia, who went out as missionaries in December, 1883. Brother Presley was a wreck with the tropical fever; Hattie, his wife, within one and a half years, together with her babe, died. Dr. Colley made the boxes in which they were laid to rest in a strange land.

They organized the Bendoo and Jundoo Mission Stations on Lake Peasue. Colley and Presley worked at Bendoo, while the single men, Brother Cole and Brother Henderson McKinney, cared for Jundoo Station on the opposite side of the lake.

Arriving in Monrovia, I preached in the First Baptist Church, founded by the heroic missionary Lott Carey. The more I became acquainted with conditions in the country, the more zealous I was to reach and preach in the outlying districts, and I tried to cover as much ground as I could with my message. At Brewerville, I found the Rev. J. O. Hayes, missionary from North Carolina, and with that station as my headquarters, evangelistic trips to many points within radius of at least 40 miles, into the "bush," were made, giving me a chance to see, taste, feel, and smell conditions in Africa. I was thus imbued with an enthusiasm for the missionary project that stood me in good stead when, eleven years later, my brethren at the National Baptist Convention called upon me to head the work of the Foreign Mission Board. I gave up a salary of $900 per year for a work without a dime in treasury and not even a lead pencil to work with, and which, by locating in Louisville, Kentucky, lost the support of its Virginia friends.

My Largest Church Building Effort

If a man could combine in himself the intelligence of a a cherub and the love of a seraph, he could not, even then, be a witness, if grace had not transformed his own soul.

The Union Baptist Church in Philadelphia, 12th Street, near Bainbridge, to which I was called in the summer of 1891, was worshiping in a basement far back from the street, and by the grace of God and the confidence secured I rallied those people until there was not standing room in the church any Sunday.

I assisted in adding 1,100 members to the church in six years, and we built what was regarded as the most extensive building of its kind owned by the group in Philadelphia. It is said that Baptists were rejuvenated and inspired. Thoughtful leaders who still live—men like Drs. E.W. Johnson, T.P. Wilson, and J.H. Duckery, insist to this day that I was a blessing to that great city. The building is still modern and is now owned by the Salem Baptist Church, Dr. Gardner, Pastor.

Later, in Pennsylvania, where I was then pastoring, I was nominated for congressman-at-large on the Prohibition ticket.

I was elected Corresponding Secretary of the Foreign Mission Board on February 13, 1896, and on entering the larger work I at once saw the need of a medium of publicity, and during March, the Board issued the Mission Herald, which had only four pages—6x9 inches. The split in 1889, in Texas, was not very old, but the leaders had been forced to take sides. Men like Drs. A.R. Griggs, I. Toliver, E.W.D. Isaac, and F.G. Davis were on one side, and Drs. R.H. Boyd, L.L. Campbell, J.A. Dennis, and E.M. Wright led the other side. I was interested, having recently lived and worked with all those men in Texas, and in my little paper I criticized them for being able to fellowship Methodists, Campbellites, and others, but not being able to work with each other. They must split churches, associations, and conventions, when "the devil and Tom Walker" were fighting them all. One day, by chance, I found in the Western Star, then published by Dr. Isaac, what I still think was one of the most beautiful editorials I have ever read. In it he told how he and David Abner, then President of Guadalupe College, had been friends from boyhood, and that their parents before them were friends, and in the Baptist controversy of Texas, they were on opposite sides, but they had vowed no matter what might happen to the Baptists, they would remain personal friends.

In the Little Herald I had also given my reason for supporting the publishing idea that was being so widely discussed and was then taking shape for Negroes to make their own literature. While I was feeling good, I wrote Dr. Isaac commending him for the very high Christian spirit exhibited in his editorial on the ties between David and himself. In one of those dry, matter-of-fact ways that characterized Dr. Isaac, he answered, "I appreciate your letter, and all I said about Abner and myself is true, but that is not going to keep me from working on your baby paper"—and he did.

But those days are all past, and although Dr. Isaac who was the author of the comment "Negro Backs and White Man's Brains," concerning our literature, four years later was fighting on my side of the question; was elected to organize our young people; and became a power for good in projecting the idea of Negro literature and leadership.

CHAPTER VI

My Education

"Whoso bears his brother's burden,
Whoso shares another's woe,
Brings his frankincense to Jesus
With the men of long ago."

—J. A. Blaisdell

N MY SPAN OF life and with such a poor start and poorer background, the largest access I have had to learning and letters came through the men, women, and phases of human existence that I have contacted. These persons had a peculiar fascination for me, and I have ever tried to find out why and how they accomplished the work they had undertaken for humanity. Early in life I met and grew to admire and love many of the sturdy old Baptist preachers who, coming "up from slavery," laid the foundation of our present denominational structure. Such men as Elders Rent Ramsey, Randall Pollard, Dan Webster,

Marion Dunbar, and H.P. Jacobs influenced me even before I left my native State of Mississippi. Hon. James Lynch, Secretary of State in Mississippi, and the first one of the group who ever served in such a place, talked to our Sunday school, the New Hope Baptist Sunday School, Meridian, Mississippi, the first one I ever saw or attended, and lastingly impressed me, shortly after my freedom.

My life was enriched because I clasped hands with such men as the scholarly Dr. William J. Simmons, Kentucky, organizer and president of Eckstein Norton University and author of *Men of Mark*; Richard DeBaptiste, Illinois, statistician and historian; Rufus L. Perry, New York, painstaking and enthusiastic historian of Baptist doings and editor of the Baptist Monitor. All of these had a part in shaping whatever has been worthwhile in my life. Yet of all who helped, I shall never forget and never cease to be especially grateful for having met with William W. Colley, organizer of the Baptist Foreign Mission Convention. The Board at Richmond had brought him home and released him in Richmond without work, and with a large family. He had gone in the woods near Clifton Forge, Virginia, was building a brush arbor and was planning for a camp meeting, under the care of the United Brethren. Dr. Thomas A. White, then pastoring in Clifton Forge, told me what Colley was doing and about where I would be likely to find him. I took the journey of one and one-half or two miles and found him working at the brush arbor, alone.

You cannot know with what joy, nor can I forget the happiness that filled my soul, when after my search for the man who had spent fourteen years in Africa, at last was found. I had been in the work four years, but for the whirlwind gait I had to go in trying to reorganize the work I would have looked him up sooner. Africa had kindled such a blaze in our denominational life and work only fourteen years before, he deserved better treatment at our hands. Toil-worn, dejected and discouraged though he was, I at once insisted that be let the brush arbor go and return to inspire the brotherhood by his presence at the twenty-first session of our National Baptist Convention, which convened in Cincinnati, Ohio, in September, 1901. Elder Colley had been grieving because he had unwittingly caused the death of a native boy, and although the Liberian government fully exonerated him by pronouncing the shot accidental, yet the Board, located at that time (1892) in Richmond, Virginia, had subjected the faithful missionary to such severe censure that his spirit quailed under the disfavor of some of his brethren, and he had withdrawn from the denomination entirely. But I asked and received permission of the Board to enter Brother Colley's name as one of the principal speakers on our program. This appearance made a profound impression. Not long after the Cincinnati meeting he was called to the pastorate of a church at Asheville, North Carolina, and labored on the home field with same earnestness that he had shown in Africa until he passed from work to reward.

Over Seas

I have been to England a dozen times. I have met and dined with Dr. John Clifford, met and visited Drs. McClaren and Hugh Brown. I have spoken in many of the larger churches, including Spurgeon's great Tabernacle, where I have preached twice. I have worshipped in John Knox's church in Scotland, and in Westminster Abbey and St. Paul's in London.

While in Liberia from time to time I met Dr. Edward D. Blyden and three of its presidents; viz., Barclay, Howard, and King. Here also I met Col. Young two years before his death. On one of these visits Knighthood was conferred upon me by President Daniel Edward Howard, by whom I was made a member of the Knight Commander of Africa's Redemption Army. I was blessed with the acquaintance of other famous men.

Organizations And Other Great Souls I Have Known

> *"Doubtless the angels would gladly have been the bearers of this good news. We are divinely told how they stand overawed before such a display of grace to sinners, and, as from the verge of some unfathomable abyss, gazed down into the depths of a love which they 'desire to look into" but cannot explore."*
>
> —Selected

Senator Blanche K. Bruce and his career as a lawmaker were a source of pride to me. James Hill, the gifted Jackson, gave me visions of the possibilities of Negroes when given a chance; Senator Hiram Revels of Holly Springs; John R. Lynch, Mississippi Representative to Congress from the long, narrow "shoestring district" in my native state, who once served as temporary chairman at a National Republican Convention; Wright Cuney of Galveston, Texas, whom men feared for his daring and respected courage; Colonel "Bill" Pledger of Atlanta, the "storm center" of many a political battle, both in Georgia and in the Washington Legislative Halls; and Samuel McElwee of Tennessee, orator, legislator, and statesman. These and men of similar spirit won and held my admiration.

When, years ago, the Federal Council of the Churches of Christ in America was taking shape, under the leadership of Dr. McFarland as the executive secretary and moving spirit, with the consent of Dr. Morris, I paid the entrance fee for the National Baptist Convention. I did this after I had visited it alone in 1905. For two years I had seen and felt that it was destined to be a power and would help our group. Outstanding laymen like Ed E. Cooper, founder and publisher of the *Freeman*, our first illustrated weekly paper of any large proportion; fighting Tim Fortune of the New York Age; Editor Murphy, founder and owner of the Afro-American; Dr. Booker T. Washington and Dr. R. R. Moton of Tuskegee, and Editor Abbott of the Defender; Editor Vann of the Pittsburgh Courier; and the Young brothers, who own the Norfolk Journal and Guide, and the Philadelphia Tribune founded by the Hon. Cris Perry and J. B. Bass of the California Eagle, were all known to me.

I have known, as intimately as a Negro who to some extent is still tainted with Southern traditions, may know the average white man, such eminent Southern white Baptists as Drs. Rufus Burleson and B. H. Carroll of Texas. It was Dr. Carroll whom we secured to deliver the main address at the cornerstone laying of New Hope Baptist Church in 1884, and I recall to this day his admonitions: "There are three things in church building about which we must never be stingy—the site, the foundation, and the roof." Many a pleasant chat I had with Dr. J.M. Frost, of the Southern Baptist Sunday School Board; Dr. R.J. Willingham of Virginia, Foreign Mission Secretary; and with Dr. E. Y. Mullins, president of the Theological Seminary, Louisville, Kentucky., who was also at one time president of the Baptist World Alliance. I knew and served on several committees with Dr. Wayland; Dr. B. Griffin, my sincere friend, pastor, and builder; and Dr. Russell H. Conwell.

The Foreign Mission Conference—this organization includes all of the Foreign Mission Boards of the United States and Canada. Drs. A.J. Brown, John R. Mott, and Robert E. Speer, were then and now among the leaders. I met the Conference yearly until the breakdown of my health in 1922. I had the privilege of attending the meeting in Garden City for this year, 1935. The warm welcomes and warm handshakes of these great leaders, their expressions of pleasure at my return to be one in their midst, I shall cherish as long as memory lasts.

When the present ruler of Abyssinia, Emperor Haile Selassie, made his noteworthy visit to the United States, he was then the only crown prince and heir-apparent to the throne. The American government domiciled him at the Waldorf-Astoria and surrounded him with all the honors and privileges due a visiting monarch. An attache representing the United States accompanied him and his entourage in all his journeys, and the respect shown the party was unstinted. I had the privilege of being presented to His Royal Highness and was most cordially received. I heard him speak through an interpreter in Metropolitan Baptist Church, W.W. Brown, Pastor. In view of the prevailing attitude of the Italian government towards the little kingdom, this meeting has furnished memories which give me a special interest and deep sympathy when the peace of the nation and its very existence are being threatened. It is a matter of history that, in 1896, Italy sent ten thousand of her crack troops under General Balmecedio against Abyssinia, and from that fatal day till now, not a single report of their activities has ever come. Not a soldier ever returned to tell what happened. Not a gun, or even a button from an Italian uniform, has ever reached the outside world. Somewhere in those hills of Abyssinia lies the secret of the reason why no dispatch, no message for relief, has been heard. Abyssinia's foes simply disappeared, men, cannon, small arms, and all—buried, like Moses, in a grave whose location God alone knows—insofar as the out-side world is concerned. The rulers of Abyssinia claimed direct descent from King Solomon, through the Queen of Sheba, and like their illustrious ancestor they do not seem to lack for wisdom.

While pastoring, I knew as personal friends Drs. I. Toliver, Charles T. Walker, James W. Carr, and George W. Lee, some of the greatest evangelists of this or any other age. For more than twenty years they ran the revival meetings for my people.

I organized and accompanied a company of our brethren as delegates to the first Baptist World Alliance ever held. It met in Exeter Hall in London.

N.B.—The Triennial Convention, made up of white Baptists, North and South, sent Lott Carey and Collin Teague to West Africa in 1821. In 1845, these white brethren split and organized the Northern and Southern Conventions. Preachers in the South wrote many books showing slavery to be right by the Bible. The war came, was fought, and ended when Baptists in both sections settled down to work again.

In 1875, the Southern Baptists sent Rev. W. W. Colley to Lagos; and after four years' stay, in November 1879, he returned. After a conference with the officers of the old Richmond African Missionary Society and pastors, the call was issued for a meeting one year later in Montgomery, Alabama, to organize a convention of Negro Baptists. More than one hundred delegates from eleven states met, and the Foreign Mission Convention of North America was organized. On December 31, 1883, they sent their first six missionaries to Liberia: Rev. W. W. Colley and his wife of Virginia; Rev. J.H. Presley and his wife of Virginia; Rev. Hence McKinney, of Mississippi; and Rev. J. J. Cole, of Virginia. Rev. Cole returned to the States about three years later to marry Miss Lucy Henry and returned to Africa, but again returned to the States as the last of their group in 1893. Because of some misunderstanding the work lagged for nearly three years but was reorganized in Atlanta, Georgia, in September 1895 (History Negro Baptists).

Forty of us went from the National Baptist Convention to help in the organization of that body, which today numbers, encourages, enlists, and enrolls Baptists the world over.

In 1910 I was among twenty delegates of the National Baptist Convention who attended the world Missionary Conference, Edinburgh, Scotland, and was present at the University of Edinburgh when both Prof. John R. Moll and Prof. Robert E. Speer received their doctorate degrees. As great souls, I have also seen and heard and known Dr. George C. Lorimer, the renowned pastor of Tremont Temple, Boston, Massachusetts, and I have spoken in the Temple. It was my privilege to see and hear that fearless and brave advocate for freedom; Henry Ward Beecher; and the Spirit-filled evangelist Dwight L. Moody. I was blessed to know and to fellowship with Dr. Weston of Crozer Seminary, Chester, Pennsylvania.

In 1887, I knew Bishop Henry M. Turner, of the

A.M.E. Church of Georgia, who proved a great friend. I served in the Afro-American Council with Bishop Alex Walters, A.M.E. Zion of New York, and with Bishop R.C. Williams, C.M.E. Bishop of Georgia. I recorded them among my personal friends. I visited the office of Recorder of Deeds, D.C., during the time of Hon. Jno. C. Dancey and C.H.J. Taylor. I met them both and knew them both as my friends.

While pastoring in Philadelphia, Pennsylvania, in 1891–96, I had such persons as Hon. Frederick Douglass, Congressman George Murray, Miss Ida B. Wells-Barnett, Robert Burdett, and also Richard Harrison to address my people. Great meetings they were.

During all my public life I secured the finest speakers and lecturers obtainable for the mental, moral, and spiritual development of my people. Drs. P.J. Bryant and W.H. Moses, both of whom were among the great of their day, said I first got them before the world in our Sunday afternoon missionary mass meetings of the National Baptist Convention.

Drs. Adam Clayton Powell of New York City, William H. Harod of Pennsylvania, pastoring our oldest and among the largest of our churches, often speak of some little kindness shown them when they were young and I was situated so I could serve them.

CHAPTER VII

Africa's Redemption: My Life's Greatest Objective

"The prospects for Foreign Missions
are as bright as the promises of God."
—Adoniram Judson

 HIRTY AND NINE YEARS ago, upon my election as Foreign Mission secretary, it became my whole duty to more fully acquaint Negro Baptists with God's claim to their service in mission fields. In those days the National Baptist Convention was bigger than its employees. The Convention domiciled its Boards, and just as a man goes to the church that calls him, the elected agent went to the home of the agency and never packed it about with him. All our trouble in 1915 grew out of a brother not obeying the orders of the National Baptist Convention. I had learned that intelligent information begets enthusiasm, and white-hot enthusiasm begets action.

I proceeded to broadcast these claims in every way I possibly could. By tongue and pen I set out facts that still hold good to this day: That Africa is a country of magnificent distances, six thousand miles long and five thousand miles wide. That it is inhabited by millions of human beings—every eighth person on this globe is of African descent; that Africa is our mother-country and therefore these are our own kith and kin, bone of our bone, flesh or our flesh; that we owe them the Gospel. With all my strength I insisted that the direct command of our Lord, "Go ye," was not optional, and that though only a few could go personally to foreign fields, many could give and all could pray.

Neglect of our opportunity to help has seemed a thing to be dreaded ever since I first found out that, along the northern coast, Africa accepted Christianity from the beginning of the Christian era, her well-organized churches were in existence before the middle of the second century, and according to Tertullian the number of Christians in the cities was about equal to that of pagans, and that in A.D. 235 a great council was held in Africa that was attended by thirty-five bishops. Why then was the faith finally stamped out? Certainly not because of the persecutions and martyrdoms that the friends of Christianity met so heroically.

It was not for lack of intellectual leadership, because of the twenty greatest names in the history of Christianity in the first four centuries after the apostles more than one half belong to Africa, among them being Origen, greatest of scholars; Clement, head of the Alexandrine college; Tertullian, the great philosopher; Augustine, Cyprian; and many other leaders. If only the leaders who followed them had devoted their time and talents to the evangelization of the vast continent which gave them birth, instead of engaging in weighty theological and philosophical discussions finally degenerating to wrangling over the problem of the "number of angels that could sit on the point of a needle," today Africa would be ablaze with the light of the gospel and "the Dark Continent" would not be a hotbed of Mohammedanism, paganism, and idolatry. Because interest in soul-saving declined, Christianity has never been able to recover the ground it lost when the church forgot her message.

I cannot rid myself of the belief that the main reason why American Negroes have been so blessed of God is that they may minister to their benighted brethren in Africa, and it was with this firm conviction I undertook and carried on the work of arousing our brotherhood in behalf of poor, sorrowing, sobbing Africa.

In 1849, the world hardly believed in East Africa there were snow-covered mountains. Ten years later, by the efforts of explorers and missionaries, the world learned there were great lakes of water in Central Africa equal to our sheets of water making up Lakes Michigan, Superior, Erie, and others between us and Canada.

In 1886, European nations owned less than one-tenth of Africa, and Portugal owned one-half of that one-tenth. Within fifty years—since the organization of our National Baptist Convention, the whole continent, except Egypt, Abyssinia, and Liberia, is controlled by Europeans, and now Abyssinia is threatened. African Christians lost their opportunity. Poor sinning, sobbing Africa is paying an awful price in sweat, tears, blood and great sorrow to hand over to nations overseas what they exact for ruling over them.

Two-thirds of the world's gold comes from Africa. Ninety per cent of its diamonds, the world gets from Africa; much of its food stuffs and cotton, European nations get from Africa. God said, "Subdue and till the earth." Not one foot of land is ours, only as we use it. The outer world needed the many great, good, and valuable things in all parts or Africa, and Africans for many reasons did not know how to market them, and so like blind Sampson she is now made to turn the mill for the help and amusement or others.

The teachings of Christ, though so frequently disobeyed, are taught by a faithful few, and despite this ugly picture, Africa is on her way up and out.

Let all who love God, love, pray for, and help Africa.

Memory of Geo. Lisle

I do not remember when the truth that the honor of being the first American Baptist foreign missionary belonged to George Lisle dawned upon me.

Previously I had unquestioning faith in the statement that Adoniram Judson was the first to go from the United States to a foreign country with the gospel message, but in the course of my delving in the subject of missions I ran across the accounts of the life and work of Lisle as narrated by early historians. Comparing the date of his sailing to the West Indies, 1783, with the date 1812, when Judson embarked for Burma, I soon discovered that Lisle had been preaching to his benighted brethren some 29 years before Judson's sailing. I was still more thrilled to find that, when William Carey, the English pioneer missionary, was still pegging away in his Molton cobbler's shop, Lisle was aggressive in his ministry to the sin-sick souls of Kingston. But it was not until 1914 that I was privileged to visit the scene of his labors.

In company with Dr. C.H. Parrish, I set out to find and lay, if possible, a flower on his grave. With much difficulty we finally located the spot where Lisle's body is said to have been buried. But the grave was empty. Only a few yards away was the marble slab which once had covered the mound, encrusted with dirt and decayed matter that took hard work and several quarts of coal oil to clean the stone so that we could photograph it. We organized a great meeting and impressed on the Baptists of Jamaica the great importance of reverencing the last resting-place of the sainted missionary. I urged that, if anyone knew where the bones of Lisle were buried, they would tell us, and if they did not care to erect a fitting memorial there in Kingston, we would see that Georgia, his native state, would do so. But it seemed there was no one still living who could give this information. No one knew where they were. On our return to the United States, we reported this fact, and out of love for this noble character the Foreign Mission Board set out to raise a fund for erecting a monument to his memory. Two years later, the annual meeting of the National Baptist Convention was held in Savannah, Georgia, with one idea paramount—that of honoring our pioneer foreign missionary, whose works follow him even though the resting-place of his ashes is not certain. In the churchyard of the First Bryan Baptist Church of Savannah, the beautiful marble shaft is still standing which was unveiled with appropriate ceremonies in September 1916.

CHAPTER VIII

Resignation of Dr. L. G. Jordan, After Serving 25 Years and 10 Months

WROTE THE FOLLOWING letter to the Chairman, Officers, and Members of the Foreign Mission Board of the National Baptist Convention I had served for so long. The time had come, I felt, to lay down the work that had occupied me for more than a quarter-century.

Philadelphia, PA, July 30, 1921

My dear Brethren:
In His Name I Greet You:
　　I hereby tender to you my resignation (D.V.) to take effect on and after Founder's Day, November 24, 1921.
　　Most of you were active in the ministry when I

gave up a prosperous pastorate in this city for this work twenty-five and one-half years ago. You know how I have toiled on without one month's vacation, though it was voted me by your goodness of heart each year. You also know how our work has grown from no recorded members in foreign fields to more than 40.000 baptized believers. and millions who hear of our work week in and week out, in the Islands of the Sea, South and Central America, and many parts of Africa.

Beginning with Rev. John Tule, in 1897, 97 persons have gone out as workers of this Board. These have ordained more than 125 native elders. More than 100 young men and women from many parts have been in this country under your Board during these 25 years. Many have finished, returned to their homes, and are doing good work. Rev. J. E. East, who has spent 11 years in Africa, is said to be available and in my judgment is well equipped by training and as a worker to enter into sympathy with the work and the workers and may do the work of a secretary. He has youth, experience, and ability for the task. With the aid of the scholarly training of Brother M.H. Jackson, our field secretary, he should make a successful executive. I pledge him, or whoever the Board selects, God helping me, every atom of my help.

You have an army or strong, well-tried, successful young pastors from whom to select a worthwhile, prayerful, godly man. For be it remembered I virtu-

ally organized our Foreign Mission work and grew with it. Of all the times in our history, you need a man now, a man with good religion, tact, strong in appeal—powerful in prayer and an executive of the first magnitude.

I have no plans for the future. I will serve anywhere except in the lead. I must not be responsible for raising the salaries of any workers—I will help.

Without a plan, my successor cannot do his best. I beg of you as members of the Board to adopt one of the plans we have recommended to the churches. Our haphazard way of raising money for missions is used nowhere and for no other purpose, and should die here and now. Do not leave the National meeting until you adopt one of our plans.

I go from you for the want of strength to go as your secretary; I go with the love and respect of my brethren, for which I praise God. If at any time I have been rash in speech, my brethren, it was in love. I meant it for our good and the good of the work.

I have tried to emphasize John Wesley's motto: "Get all you can without hurting your soul, your body, or your neighbor. Save all you can, cutting off every needless expense. Give all you can; be glad to give and ready to distribute; laying up in store for yourselves good foundations against the time to come, that ye may attain eternal life."

I know that according to the Scripture, we are not true to God or to our profession when we can organize people to buy houses, lands, autos, and what-not for our personal use, and cannot organize them to raise $100.00 in a whole year to save the whole non-Christian world—there is something wrong with our hearts. My brethren, the wrong of neglecting the Kingdom, the sin of forgetting our Lord's last command, will bring its punishment on us or our children. There is no escape.

I know each of you know, like Pettiford and Wilhite, of Alabama; Robinson of Arkansas, Vann of Tennessee; Hayes of Virginia; Dupree of Kentucky; and our own Charles T. Walker of Georgia must go over this river. Like Isaac, I do beg that we all deal kindly with our Master, in this matter of Foreign Missions.

And now, may the God of all grace bless each of you in your homes, your pastorates, and as members of the most important Board of our Great Convention is the prayer and wish of,

Yours in his service,
L. G. Jordan

(Journal National Baptist Convention, Page 188, 1921)

The Going of Dr. Jordan

The Executive Committee of the Foreign Mission Board of the National Baptist Convention:

In receiving for transmission to the Foreign Mission Board and on to the National Baptist Convention the resignation of Rev. L. G. Jordan, D. D., we do so with feelings of sorrow, regret, and deep prayerful sympathy. There has not been but one Jordan; his equal will be hard to find.

He came to the service of our great Convention and of our Saviour for the redemption of Africa and of the foreign fields more than twenty-five years ago, while yet young, strong, active and full of hopeful vision and plans for the work which lay before him. His activities and accomplishments have been marvelous; he has been a torch-light, blessing both his and all other strong Negro religious denominations in centering their minds and efforts upon world-wide missions and inaugurating and putting into executive plans and methods which have wrought wonders for our Lord and Master. His endurance and resourcefulness have puzzled many of us.

Leaving the pastorate of one of the very best churches in the denomination, entering upon the work which at that time seemed chaotic and almost hopeless, he has brought hope out of confusion and light out of darkness, so that today it is no longer a question of the possibility of the redemption of Africa and other foreign fields but simply means missionaries and work. Dr. Jordan has given his all—strength, intelligence, and earthly possessions for the extension of the Master's kingdom in foreign lands.

As he goes from us, a worn-out body appeals to us in acquiescing in his retirement, officially, from the duties of his position. We recommend, therefore, *that he be retired as secretary emeritus, upon a pension or a salary of $1,200.00 per year with the privilege of membership in this Board during the remainder of his natural life.*

Aaron R. Robinson, Chairman
Wesley F. Graham, Treasurer
Jacob R. Bennett, Rec. Secretary

The above was passed by the Foreign Mission Board on July 30, 1921, reported to the National Baptist Convention, and adopted by it September 9, 1921, at Chicago, 14 years ago. I will call upon my brethren and sisters everywhere to witness before God if I have kept my word during these 14 years that have lapsed since this resignation was offered and reluctantly received by the brotherhood.

The late Dr. East, my successor at the National Baptist Convention sessions both in Ohio and in Missouri, gave his opinion of me.

Dr. East often said that the most happy stroke of my official career was in locating the Foreign Mission Board in Philadelphia, so close to the sailing point, New York, and the returning point of all missionaries. I do not know of anything that has given me more cheer than another statement of Dr. East, in which he gave me credit in the following words: "Dr. Jordan, each of the main stations in Africa are located at strategic points. They could not have been located better. Your far-sightedness is displayed in the location of these stations more than anything else in your career."

In one of the last letters I received from him, Dr. East, while he was sick, said, "You are the father of our foreign mission work; pray for us and tighten your traces and help the work all you can."

I wrote members of our Foreign Mission Board, "No selfish or sinful act to the injury of any of my brethren is charged against me. Now that Dr. J.E. East, our secretary, is dead, and I am fairly well and active, am I a sinner because I say through the goodness of God and my prayerful study of missions I believe the foreign mission work will be helped if I am allowed to fill the unexpired term of Dr. East, giving our Board time to look about and wisely select a permanent corresponding secretary?" Is anyone wronged, or mistreated, when I reiterate with the consent of the Foreign Mission Board that the Mission Herald was organized and dedicated by me in March 1896?
Also that I planned and fathered the organization of the Providence Industrial Mission in Central Africa, where Miss Delaney labored for five years, Rev. L.N. Cheek spent seven years, and where Rev. John Chilembee, the organizer, was murdered in 1914?

"The Buchanan mission at Middledrift, South Africa, organized by Rev. Joseph I. Buchanan, dedicated by the writer in 1904, and where Dr. J. E. East labored for 11 years; also the Bible Industrial Mission Station on the St. John River, 14 miles from Grand Bassa, organized by Miss Susie M. Taylor and where Miss Eliza L. Davis, Miss Priscilla Bryant, Rev. D.R. Horton and wife, Dr. Sykes, also Dr. Robert M. Sisusa and wife worked from one to sixteen years each, also the Suehn Mission 40 miles up the St. Paul River in Liberia, organized by Miss E.B. Delaney in 1912, and which I dedicated in 1920; to this station has gone Miss Sarah Williamson (now Mrs. Shields), Miss Ruth Morris, Dr. Hubbard, and other well-equipped workers; these main outstanding stations are situated on from 90 to 300 acres of land, all of which were organized and on which good corrugated iron buildings were erected and the work set in good running order before I resigned on account of ill health in September, 1921.

"I also planned for our mission headquarters in Philadelphia, bought, remodeled, and paid for it through a bequest of Miss C.G. Ewen, of New York, without it costing our denomination a ten-cent piece. I appealed to this good woman, interested her in our work and made a friend of her for Africa. The last year I served as secretary of the Board, our Baptist people contributed to African missions through me nearly forty thousand dollars.

"Note Auditor Pierson's *Report* on page 204 1931 *Journal*."

CHAPTER IX

My Last Official Trip to Africa

N 1920, WHEN ON my last visit to Africa I baptized 19 converts at Suehn (the word for trips in West Africa is "dash"), the young African who took my wet clothes to hang out, with a big laugh said, "Daddy, you love me?"

I said "Yes, I am here because my people across the sea and I love you."

He said, "*Dasha me dese*," and I did. Everywhere you turn it is "Dasha me" something or other. So I "dashed" until I hardly had a handkerchief or pair of socks when I came home. On Monday, I went out to help our boys clean some land. Laid off my hat and coat and went at it with a sharp machete. Soon I saw the boys running away. I looked to see what had happened, and then they pointed to a yellow-jacket nest that a few more strokes would bring down on my head. In Africa they build their nests of mud in trees 5 or 7 feet from the ground. As I looked and saw the nest, and possibly 500 of these little warriors that had been summoned to the outside by their sentinels to get me, did I run? Yes, indeed, wishing I could fly. Nothing in my whole life's work is more cheering than the part I had in helping our foreign students. I brought nine from South Africa in 1904, two of whom climbed through grammar grades, high school, and college afterwards, graduating as doctors of medicine.

In 1917, I brought four from West Africa, and in 1920 I brought five. Many others came alone during the 25 years, so that more than 100 came, and nearly every Baptist school educated or partly educated from one to four of these searchers for knowledge, and they are now serving their people in Central, South, and West Africa. These are the assets of my more than 40 years' work for our Motherland, Africa.

When I resigned on July 1, 1921, the churches had given to our Board during the current year:

Total receipts, year ending July 1, 1921,	$39,931.35
Money due missionaries	1,759.28
Money due on mortgage	2,100.00
Balance due retiring Secretary Jordan	2,275.97

"I Went to Pieces Sure Enough"

"Find out the plan of God in your day; and then beware that you do not cross it, but fall into your own place in that plan."

—Prince Albert.

For over two years before my resignation, I was conscious that I was gradually undermining my health, and that I ought to rest, but saw neither time nor place to take a vacation from the strain of a quarter of a century of responsibility. It was in 1922, while attending The Federal Council in Indianapolis, Indiana, and stopping with the late Dr. B.J.F. Wesbrook, I was sitting early one morning talking to Rev. Borders, father of Dr. H.T. Borders, of Newark, New Jersey, when to all appearances I died.

Greatly frightened, he hurried from the room and summoned the family, saying, "Dr. Jordan is dead." I am told that the men folks gathered about me and began saying, "Poor Brother Jordan is gone."

But Mrs. Wesbrook would not trust appearances, but insisted that Dr. C.H. Johnson, who happened up in his car, should get a physician. He hastily summoned Dr. W.E. Brown, my friend. While all this was taking place, Mrs. Wesbrook had secured a towel and cold water and bathed my face and insisted on the preachers lifting my arms up and down as in treatment for drowned persons. By this time the doctor had arrived and began to work on me. With strychnine pumped in my heart, I revived, and though very weak for weeks, thank God, I lived on. The late Dr. P. James Bryant saw to it that no mention was made to me of the death of Dr. W.G. Parks, which had occurred the day before my collapse. When I got better, Dr. L.K. Williams came from Chicago and carried me to the home of one of his deacons, Mr. James Clark, where I remained until I was able to travel alone. For nearly ten years, I was slowly coming back, and now I praise God for excellent health for a man of my years, and that my interest in public affairs is unabated; I travel still continually and preach every Sunday and many week nights. In Dr. Morris' last address before the National Baptist Convention, he recommended a corresponding secretary for the Convention, and constitutional provisions were made for such an official. I was selected, but served only two years, as the plan did not suit the secretary or the National Baptist Convention. Of course in my judgment such an official is still needed. Complaint is often made that, in our day, public servants among Negro Baptists very soon get bigger than their jobs and then become dictators, thereby causing misunderstandings, stagnation, and often decay in the objectives we are trying to reach. Dr. Rushbrook of the World Baptist Alliance is a good illustration of such a need.

To make myself understood the following self-explanatory letter was sent to a few friends:

701 South 19th Street
Philadelphia, Pennsylvania
October 20, 1934

My dear Brother:
    Thirteen years ago, the 24th of next month, I gave up the Foreign Mission work after I had spent nearly twenty-six years at it. Now that Dr. East, my

successor, is dead, a lull in our work will most likely follow. More than 100 of our best men have asked that I return to the Board. Men like Drs. Nabrit, Ga.; Robinson, Ala.; Gayden, Miss.; Branham, and a committee of brethren from Illinois. I had not thought of it until importuned by these men. When I recall that I planned for, named, and issued the Mission Herald, March 1896, and every Main Station we have in Africa and elsewhere was organized and located while I served, also planned for, bought, remodeled, and paid for our Foreign Mission rooms, 701 S. 19th Street, from money which was really willed to me by a good white friend, I am asking that the Board call me to fill the unexpired term of the late Dr. East. Indeed I feel because of my large experience and long service, my denomination can well afford to grant this desire. The late Dr. East said on more than one occasion, "Dr. Jordan has made the largest contribution to foreign work of the group than any man living or dead." The selection of a successor to the late Dr. East belongs to the Foreign Mission Board, and, I feel, using me to fill the unexpired term, or until the time or selecting a permanent corresponding secretary, you will have a part in it, hence this letter.

I understand the Board meets on the 24th, in Philadelphia, so if you feel that I am worthy, and my request reasonable, please be on hand or hasten your proxy to the Board. Write me your reaction at any rate.

Hoping you and yours are well, I am,
Yours in his service,
       L.G. Jordan
      Secretary Emeritus–Historian

The Alabama State Convention had endorsed Dr. Roland Smith and more than a dozen of our best men— prepared men of the younger set; men who had been helpful and loyal to the cause of foreign missions were aspirants. The *VOICE* reported over a dozen applicants. I knew then as I know now, this is a young man's age, and out of my love for the work and our beloved denomination, I only wished to keep things together for the unexpired time.

CHAPTER X

What Others Say of Brother Jordan for the Unexpired Term

HO DOES NOT KNOW Secretary Jordan?" For more than two decades as pastor, lecturer, and secretary, prolific of plans and intolerant of opposition, of dogged persistence and courageous aggressiveness, energy tireless and love universal, North, East, South and West, he has gone, seemingly to say:

> "To serve the present age,
> My calling to fulfill.
> Oh! may it all my powers engage,
> To do the Master's will."

"That the earth should become the Lord's in the coming generation seems to be a possibility that cheers and a goal that draws him. Content to spend time, nerve force, brain fiber, gifts material and gifts spiritual for Africa especially, he is giving his zenith days, matured intellect, and ripest experience toward the development and discipline of the brethren at home, and the establishment of the kingdom or heaven and its maintenance abroad."

—*From the Introduction of* Up the Ladder in Missions, *1909, John H. Frank, M.D., D.D., first Chairman Foreign Mission Board under its present form.*

When I asked to be allowed to fill the unexpired term, two state conventions, several ministers' conferences, and a number or newspapers gave me the benefit of their good names and the use of their columns, but none was so fulsome as the following:

Doctor L.G. Jordan Neglected

"Dr. L.G. Jordan, the veteran minister and missionary, has been blessed by Providence with a long and healthy life. He is able with all his faculties of thought and experience. He could, at least, be asked to finish out the unexpired term of office caused by the passing of Dr. J. E. East. He understands the work as well as any living man in America. His years should be no barrier to his efficiency.

"The *Christian Review* makes this humble request on his behalf. We hope the powers that be may be able to see the wisdom or such a move, and as the Nestor of Baptist history and missions to serve until a successor has been faithfully sought and found. The work of foreign missions would receive the ripeness of his wis dom, the fruitage of his long years of service, and the stamp of expert knowledge from a man whose name is a household word in Baptist circles.

"Many years ago he stood at the inception of this noble department of the National Baptist Convention. He was the doctor at its birth and nourished it to national power. He has faithfully served his day and generation worthily enough to have something to do along missionary endeavors as long as life lasts. He should not be forced to speak for himself. Men now, who were boys when Dr. Jordan was younger, can see the grandeur of his life and services to missions.

"In the Foreign Mission Offices in Philadelphia this noble sire, this Baptist historian, this returned missionary from Africa, this humanitarian for the heathen, this guide of the destiny of the Baptist cause in America, this friend to the friendless, Dr. L.G. Jordan, would honor the position, and those who would grant him the opportunity to serve, would do honor to themselves and their Master."

—*from the Christian Review*

Excerpts Taken at Random
from Letters Received from Friends

DALLAS, TEXAS

It is my sincere hope that the denomination will exercise the good judgment to secure your services for a period at least so that someone who has knowledge of the work can hold the reins while matters are so in-

definite, and while the place is being sought by so many
who have shown little fitness and who have no definite
knowledge of the work and the proper methods to be
used for its furtherance.

—*Maynard H. Jackson*

HELENA, ARKANSAS

I cast my vote for you. Sure you know more about
the work than any minister I now. Hope the brethren
will agree and let you have your request.

—*H.R. Stephenson.*

FORT SMITH, ARKANSAS

I would like very much to be there and cast my vote
for you. . .I am very sorry proxies will not be accepted.
Dr. Adams wrote me they would not. . .but if they
change, my vote is for you.

—*William Erby*

NEW HAVEN, CONNECTICUT

Since it will be impossible for me to be present at your
meeting to select someone to fill the unexpired term of the
late Dr. J.E. East, I cast my ballot for Dr. L.G. Jordan.

—*John B. Pharr*

DENVER, COLORADO

I am highly in favor of the election of Dr. L.G. Jordan to carry out unexpired time of the late Dr. J.E. East.
Because of Dr. Jordan's previous achievements and
broad experience in our Foreign Mission work I believe
he is the right man for the place.

—*T.S. Saunders*

WASHINGTON, D.C.

I think you would be a fine man to carry on the work of the Board until the meeting of the Convention.

—*W.H. Jernagin*

DES MOINES, IOWA

I regret very much the untimely death of Dr. East. You should be allowed to take up the the work pending the selection or another person. Everything possible is in your favor.

—*J. W. Tutt*

DAYTON, OHIO

The successor of Dr. East should be a man who is familiar with the work because these trying times through which we are passing demand the services of the man who would be equal to the emergency.

—*Ernest C. Estell*

ST. PAUL, MINNESOTA

I am very much interested in the selection of a corresponding secretory from the Foreign Mission Board. I am sure that it would be timely for you to fill out the unexpired term; and more, it seems that to take up a man and put him on the field without anyone to aid him would retard the work. I favor the proposition as mentioned by many of the brethren, that you fill out the unexpired term, and at the same time select a man who would be an asset to any worker.

—*L. W. Harris*

SHREVEPORT, LOUISIANA

As soon as I heard of the home going of Dr. East, I discussed with some of the brethren that you would be the logical one for the position because of your long experience.

—*L. Allen*

LEXINGTON, MISSISSIPPI

I feel that justice would be done the cause by appointing Dr. Jordan to fill the unexpired term, a man who knows the work alphabetically.

—*Rev. I.S. Pettus*

KANSAS CITY, MISSOURI

I vote (by proxy) for Rev. L. G. Jordan for corresponding secretary.

—*J. P. Holmes*

SIOUX FALLS, SOUTH DAKOTA

I class you as one of the outstanding men in our race, and as a source of guidance and direction to those of our Baptist cause that are being sponsored by the National Baptist Convention.

—*M.W. Withers*

WHITE SULPHUR SPRINGS, WEST VIRGINIA

I am quite sure with your past experience and ripe knowledge of the foreign field, you would be the plausible person not only for the unexpired term, but would be suited for the permanent corresponding secretary.

—*William Jackson*

DENNISON, TEXAS

You know the work perhaps as no other man knows it at this time.

—*Joseph A. Brown.*

LOUISVILLE, KENTUCKY

To this end I have witnessed Rev. Jordan plead till the feelings of his soul rose to tears in his eyes and he sank down to his chair, sobbing out the love that bound him to the unenlightened "from far away," and that makes his words so mighty to move the thousands that hang upon his lips, lips that at times seem touched with fire not of earth. And who hearing him doubts the reality of the unseen Christ, the imperative need of the lost soul, the unquestioned right of the missionary to be heard, the glorious triumphs of the cross, the possibility of the immediate conversion of the whole world to Jesus Christ our Lord?

—*John H. Frank, M.D., D.D., in 1909*

The Secretary Elected

At the Louisville Board Meeting, December 12, 1934, Rev. J.L. Jackson was elected corresponding secretary for our Foreign Mission Board, following which action, Dr. L.K. Williams showed a fine spirit of fair play and increased the love and admiration which the brethren had for him by the following statement:

"Brethren, the eyes of the country are upon us

today, and I sincerely wish you would use Dr. Jordan as associate or helper to our young secretary. It will be a mistake on our part if we fail to use Dr. Jordan in this capacity. He has expressed himself as wishing to help in this work. I think he should be allowed this privilege. There is not a man in all the country that knows the Foreign Mission work as does Dr. Jordan. I have had a number of letters from brethren over the country, respecting our using Dr. Jordan. He has been overseas four times and is thoroughly prepared to cope with the situation both in America and in Africa. Men like Dr. R.T. Pollard, Alabama; Dr. A.C. Powell and G.H. Simms, New York; Dr. J.R. Jamison of Arkansas; Dr. T.O. Fuller of Tennessee; and many others who are loyal to this cause are listening to hear from this meeting. This matter can be equalized in such a way as to bring about harmony and great good to the cause of Christ. Remember that the cause is the Lord's, let him be glorified."

Following these remarks, Dr. C.C. Adams, Chairman of the Foreign Mission Board, quickly and cheerfully made a motion that Dr. Jordan be elected as associate corresponding secretary of the Foreign Mission Board, and it was warmly seconded by Dr. P.H. Hughes, treasurer of the Board, and adopted by the Board of Directors and Mission Board jointly.

As shown by pulpit and press, the denomination was ready that I fill the unexpired term, but for some reason the Philadelphia brethren disclaimed any unex-

pired term and pushed the election of a permanent corresponding secretary, which was acceded to out of in
deference to their wishes.

The Aftermath Of It

WASHINGTON, D.C.

I congratulate you on being returned to the work
you love and to which you have given your very best.

—*N.H. Burroughs*

GEORGIA

"I have just read in the National Baptist Voice of
your appointment as associate corresponding secretary
of the Foreign Mission Board of th National Baptist
Conference, U. S. A. I want to congratulate you and
the National Baptist Convention on this movement.
It seems fitting that you should be back with the Board,
having had forty years of experience, and having the
grasp of historical information concerning your Convention and its Board. Associated with a young man
of such prominence as Dr. Jackson seems to be, I think
it wonderful for the cause."

—*Noble Y. Beall (Home Mission Board*
of the Southern Baptist Convention)

TENNESSEE

We elected Dr. L. G. Jordan, historian of the National Baptist Convention, as an assistant to the Rev.
J.H. Jackson. The young men of the denomination

felt that youth and maturity should be linked together; that Dr. Jordan had done too much for the
Baptist denomination to be brushed aside without
consideration. President Williams led the way in per-
fecting that happy combination of a brilliant, youthful
leader, on the one hand, and a battle-scarred veteran
on the other—working together to redeem the "bleeding sore of the world."

—*The National Baptist Voice.*

TYLER, TEXAS

I am out of the schoolroom for just a few days.
Being in my den and looking through some books, I
came to your book *Up the Ladder in Missions,* and I
began to look through it anew. It is worth its weight
in any kind of money and should be put into a better
binding and used as a textbook in any school of religion on "Foreign Missions." It seems that the city of
Philadelphia is a fine place from which to select Foreign Mission secretaries. You came to that office
from the Union Baptist Church to succeed Rev. L.M.
Luke, and Dr. Jackson is also from that city and also
an old Mississippian, and so are you. It is a fine thing
to have you with him, for you will be of much help to
him.

—*A.T. Stewart*

PENNSYLVANIA

I must send a note at least in response to your good
letter of the 10th, with congratulations that you are held
in honor by your associated brethren of the National

Baptist Convention, and are not burdened by them as largely as at first seemed possible.

I am now expecting rather definitely to get the books together sometime this week, and ship them to you. As soon as I can do that, I will write again.

Very cordially yours,

Frank G. Lewis
Librarian,
American Baptist Historical Society

CHAPTER XI

Some Things With Which I Agree

*"People will not look forward to posterity who
never look backward to their ancestors."*
—*Edmund Burke*

R. CHARLES SATCHEL MORRIS used to say,
"Brother Jordan pleads for Africa with the
fondness of an ardent lover." At our Baptist
Convention at Chicago, in 1905, at the close of our appeal for Africa, Dr. E.J. Fisher arose and came across
th pulpit, saying, "I donate my horse and buggy."
Rev. Sparks, who still lives and works in New York,
came from the rear of the church and put his watch
and chain in the collection. At our meeting at
Newark, New Jersey, in 1919, with President John
Hope heading our Committee on Finance, the people
laid $4,011.01 on the able. All praise to Jesus, who
taught me to love Africa, and to this day my heart
goes out to that land.

Hats Off! Coats Off!

"Hats off to the past! Coats off to the future!" exclaimed Dan Crawford. Never did we need that as the slogan of all Christians more than at this hour. Hats off to those from whom we received our heritage. "Other men have labored, and ye are entered into their labors. "Coats off to the future!" The world will read our answer in our deeds. Where is your coat? Off with it and get busy.

—Watchman-Examiner

Speedy Spending

The Reader's Digest for June is authority for the statement that the United States News recently gave a full page to two comparative statistics. It was shown that the total expenditures of the United States from 1789 to July 1913, a period of 124 years, with four wars included, were $24,500,000,000. From July 1933 to July 1936, expenditures actual and budgeted will equal $24,200,000,000. In three years the government has spent nearly as much as had been spent during the previous 124 years, including the cost of four wars.

This is spending with a vengeance!

—Selected

The gospel ministry is not a learned profession into which men may go at their own option or at the

beck of avarice or ambition. It is a divine vocation
to which men are called by the voice of an Indwelling
Spirit, who qualifies them to bear witness for God.
No man, however gifted or learned, is competent to
preach, except insofar as the truth he proclaims is the
girdle that firmly and closely embraces his very vitals
and holds in place all his other armor.

—A.T. *Pierson*

On September 12, 1873, I was licensed to preach; was
ordained November 1874 at Cottonwood, near Lake
Providence, Louisiana; and I entered the pastorate of
my first church, Mt. Vernon, Yazoo City, Mississippi,
in 1875. Feeling keenly the need of more preparation, I
entered Roger Williams University in 1879; Dr. D.W.
Phillips was president and Dr. L.B. Tefft dean. In 1883
I went to Texas and at different times pastored Second
Baptist Church in San Antonia, New Hope in Waco,
First Church in Anderson, and St. Emanuel, Hearne.
At each of these places I planned and led in building
some of the best churches of that day.

In 1921, crushed by the incessant travel and grind
and the wear-and-tear resulting from forty-eight years'
nerve-trying work, at our Chicago meeting I resigned
from the Foreign Mission work amid the regrets and
sobs of many of our brethren. Out of respect and what
seemed to me great love for my devoted service, the
brotherhood provided for what we all thought were my
few remaining days. First, they voted that I should be
secretary emeritus—the first of which we have any

record in the work of our group. Then, for the "rainy day" whose clouds seemed to loom near, they voted that I should receive a pension of $100.00 per month as long as I lived. After three years had passed, I began to recover my strength and hence, at our Indianapolis Board Meeting, I suggested to the Board through Secretary East and Chairman Austin that they pay only $50.00 per month while I was able to earn anything in other ways, giving them permission to use the other $50.00 as my contribution to the cause of Foreign Missions.

Later on I was made historiographer of the Convention at $1,800.00 per year, and I prepared the Standard Baptist Directory and Busy Pastor's Guide, for which services the Sunday School Publishing Board canceled an indebtedness of $500.00 against me for printing, though most of the debt had been incurred in setting up the Historical Department.

By the summer of 1930, The History of Negro Baptists was hurriedly completed and published in time for our Golden Jubilee Anniversary. During this time, the Sunday School Board paid me $50.00 per month, and the National Baptist Convention from $100.00 to $300.00 per year.

This, with what I was able to pick up as I went from place to place in search of history material, caused the Convention's debt to me to grow larger each year. Now to relieve the strain I am under, and to help the Convention as well, I have settled the entire account, $6,790.43, for $2,000.00, and half that sum is in bonds, now being sold by the Refinancing Commission. Please God, I am still ready for sacrifice and service anywhere, but most of all for the sake of poor, sinning, sorrowing Africa. While I was secretary of our Foreign Mission Board, I was compelled to put up my watch on three different occasions as security, when funds were lacking, and once even my piano, to further the mission work of our denomination, and I would gladly do so again if necessary. My watch, my coat, and my life are at my Father's disposal. My work being all pioneering and laying foundations, it having fallen to my lot to pay the back salaries of my predecessors in churches, to build up-to-date church houses in five different cities in 25 years, and, with a salary of from $15.00 to $35.00 a month, there was little chance to save anything for my old age. For 10 of the best years of my life, I received from $40.00 to $60.00; the last two years of my pastorate, I got $75.00 per month; then for 25 years as secretary of our Foreign Mission Board I received from $900 to $2,000 per year. In many a crisis I have donated most of this to make the work go. The only time I ever had $1,003.00 in the bank was in 1920, when the Women's Convention was in a great strait at the Training School and I loaned them $1000.00. They paid a part of it back and then set about discussing whether the school owed this or whether it was the debt of the Women's Convention, Auxiliary to the National Baptist Convention, or the trustees of the Training School. So for more than 5 years nothing has been paid on either principal or interest. Of course it is said they pay committees, and are able to make donations, but cannot decide who owes me. This is not the honest thing to do, and I am waiting to see how long it can continue. Once, while pressing my claim for fairer treatment, I told Secretary Hudson how unjustly I was being treated while at the same time he and other officers got what was due them, and yet each made good salaries at home, while I was depending on my public work for the denomination to support myself and my family; and he replied, "If I did not get mine as I go along, I would be like you." Recently good Dr. Townsend told me I was too liberal. I believe God has given me 62 years of active service among my brethren with only one month of real incapacity from sickness, and I am, if not a good listener, at least a "jam up" good loser for a good cause.

It is said that I am generous with what I get hold of; not resentful for wrongs done me and over-trustful of people and especially my friends. Regarded as a good story-teller and apt at applying the moral—not so bad—eh!

Today I find myself ex-pastor of six churches, and ex-corresponding secretary of the Foreign Mission Board of the National Baptist Convention. By the grace of God and indefatigable self-forgetfulness, I built 6 of church houses of my day, and I left each church packed with people. In only one case did my successor become embittered over my popularity and show it. In every case I resigned over the protest of my people. I urged that they "never send for me to preach funerals or marry people, since I feel that is a pastor's duty." During over 62 years as a minister, no matter how urgent the call or how tender the ties, I have never gone back to a field or in any way made the burden of my successor heavier, nor have I ever split any work or in any way encouraged a split. I may also lay claim as ex-pastor of the Mt. Carmel Baptist Church, Philadelphia, Pennsylvania.

CHAPTER XII

"He always wins who sides with God,
To him no chance is lost."

URING THE TWENTY-FIVE years I was secretary of the Foreign Mission Board I made a trip of inspection to Demerara, South America.

For seven consecutive years the churches had been called upon to send those who felt called of God to foreign fields. January 11th, Rev. J.W. Anderson, with his family, returned to Demarara. On the 15th. Miss E.B. Delaney sailed for Chiradzulu, B.C. Africa, and on the 18th Rev. H.N. Bouey, D.D., with his three boys, sailed for Liberia, W.C. Africa. The sailing of workers has always been a source of education and inspiration to the churches.

Men and women weep for joy at the meetings as we take the parting hand and become co-workers with God in the salvation of their heathen brethren.

We rejoice to know that, during the past seven years, our Foreign Mission work has grown from the name to a fixed part of our denominational life. During this time quite sixty churches have been organized in "regions beyond," and nearly 5,000 persons have been baptized and enrolled in the army en route for the Better Land. Negro Baptists raised and expended for Foreign Missions during that time more than $43,000.00. Mail from various parts of Africa comes to the Board continually, and more and more the people of African descent everywhere are getting in line for greater work in saving each other—Journal, 1902.

During my visit to these foreign parts I visited St. Thomas, St. Croix, St. Christopher, Antigua, Guadalupe, Martinique, St. Lucia, St. Vincent, and Barbados.

It will be recalled that possibly the most disastrous earthquake in the Western Hemisphere occurred at Martinique.

Just a month after it occurred the ship on which we sailed dropped anchor in the bay. In the hospitals, in the adjacent islands, there were hundreds recovering from burns received at the terrible catastrophe. It was nothing to see men and women with the skin on the soles or their feet and the palms or their hands come off in great flakes, and the new skin pushing its way felt and looked just like the skin of a new babe. It is possibly one or the saddest occurrences of the decade, this earthquake.

The deck of our ship was covered with sand from

this earthquake. For miles away the smaller islands in the Carribbean Sea and for quite a distance beyond were fertilized by this dirt erupted. Better cane and crops of all kinds were grown because of the ashes blown from Mt. Pele, the spewing mountain from Martinique.

All of our missionaries in the islands were doing well. We organized the South America and West Indian Baptist Convention with J. W. Anderson as corresponding secretary; this was held in the Salem Baptist Church, T. E. Smith, pastor, Barbados, B.W.I.

Palm Trees

On all of the islands of South America there are palm trees, but they only seemed to be cared for because of their beauty. But when you come to the West African Boundary you will find the oil palm tree, which is said to be the most valuable of trees, and there are nearly sixty useful products from the palm tree. Palm butter, palm oil, palm cabbage with fibers and hammocks and cloth and so many other things come from this valuable tree. A writer of the wealth of West Africa says, "Any person who has 500 palm trees is rich."

One day I sat on the porch of our boy's building at our Suehn Mission Station and counted more than 100 palm trees in a radius of less than one-half mile around the station, and on the hundreds of acres belonging to the station were possibly 10,000 palm trees. The palm oil is the staple fat of that part of the world. When first taken from the palm nut it is the color of our tomato sauce, but when put into a pan and properly cooked it will then have the appearance of oil or fried meat grease. During this process it must be done outdoors; otherwise the fumes will almost choke you.

Driver Ants

The ants of West Africa are one of the evils to be combated. These ants are in size from the tiniest sugar ant to the largest red ant of Texas in the West. They travel about in droves. They are called driver ants; they make up a row in travel as large as a lead pencil, with a sentinel on each side. If they come to a house, no amount of hot water can stop them; the only thing is to take your belongings and get out of the way. When they come into the house they destroy other insects, anything edible, and if you have sick they destroy them as well. The great boa-constrictor, python, tiger, leopard, indeed anything that moves about, takes great care to avoid the drivers.

Animals

In South Africa, Dr. Livingstone combated with the lion. I never saw many vicious animals while in South America. In West Africa I saw the leopard and the bobcat. I saw only a few snakes, but they were small, and I was constantly on the lookout for a boa-constrictor.

I shall always remember one dark night traveling from Wazana to our mission station near Fortsville. We had one-half night of it in a native path. Their plan is that the visitor walk in front; the caravan with your belongings follows. The night was very dark, and we came to a ravine across which was a small foot log, and because I was tired I fell from the foot log, expecting to hit the water, but to my surprise there was only a ditch about three feet deep. I recalled always carrying a good gun to protect myself, as this country was infested with leopards, but after a while

I remembered that the nights were so dark that the animal could destroy me before I could get to my gun, so I put the gun up and trusted in the Lord.

Funerals

The helplessness and hopelessness of heathenism as seen at funerals is the saddest thing imaginable. They beat the wind and bemourn their loss without any hope of ever meeting again. The Kru people will put a corpse in a box and start for the graveyard; every now and then they will back and jerk, saying, "He no want to go, he no want to get in the grave." Just what a live person will say they say for the dead person, and very often they go round and round in the same space and carry the corpse back to the hut. I am told that the Liberian Government passed a law to make them bury their dead.

At Sierra Leone, right under the window in a home where I was stopping, I heard the wail of the sorrowing

Africans the whole night through; when day broke, they silently went about their business, and a few of them carried their friend to the graveyard. Often at the death of a friend, the hut in which they live is torn down, and again, to save the hut, the sick person they are reasonably sure they will die is dragged in the yard, so they will not die in the hut. I remember meeting a man carrying a sick man who was sure to die. The sick man was on the carrier's back with his hands locked over the carrier's forehead. The carrier, as I recollect, had taken the sick man's feet up by putting his shins in the carrier's hands. It looked as if it was one man with two heads, and my attention was attracted to the peculiar looking person. When they came nearer I got to see the hands locked across the forehead, but it did not occur to me that there were two men. When they were still nearer, my guide explained it was a sick man being carried to the sick bush. The sick bush was any bush far enough from the native town so that his spirit would not disturb the natives.

The sick man was left beside the tree, without a crust of bread or a drop of water or an ounce of medicine, to die alone, and possibly his body to be devoured by the drivers or the leopards.

It was about 3 o'clock in the afternoon when I saw this sight, and really when my eyes were closed for the night the sight of the man being carried to the sick bush behind disturbed me. Oh how I thanked God that I live in a land where there are drug stores, doctors, nurses, and hospitals.

Coffee

At our Bassa Industrial Mission, when Miss Taylor began working in 1912 she wrote to us for help in planting 11,000 coffee trees. A coffee tree requires five years for growth to maturity. It will bear a few berries before then, but it is supposed to be at the peak of itself after five years. These trees look very much like our peach trees, only the leaves are a little larger. The blossoms are as white as snow and as fragrant as jasmine. The coffee bean when raised is about the size of, and look very much like, purple red cherries, and possibly there is nothing as sweet as the juice of that berry, but when I was there no use was made of it. The bean is broken, and the two little grains of coffee in each berry face each other in a pulp that looks very much like the pulp of a muscadine or our large grapes. This bean is dried, and there is a thin hull shed from it, leaving the bean ready for market.

There are coffee trees at all our stations in Liberia, but at the Bible Industrial Mission coffee growing was made a specialty.

In 1909, I prepared *Up the Ladder in Missions*, which did as much to awaken interest in our work as the *Mission Herald* did in 1896. I had a number of our leaders write extracts on the following subjects, with illustrations of what we were trying to describe: "The General Agent, or the Topmost Needs in Missions," C.L. Fisher, D.D.; "Africa Awaiting," C.S. Morris; "How the Material Growth of Baptists Should or Would Affect the Race in America and Africa," Richard DeBaptist.

A number of men prepared sketches of sermons like the following: "Sent by Christ," W. P. Dixon—Text, John 20: 21; "Christ the Crucified—the Magnetic Attraction of the World"—C. T. Walker, D.D.—Text, John 12:32; "Our Obligation to the Heathen," Rev. Mark Thomas, A. M.—Text, Romans 1:14, 15; "Authority for Missions at Home and Abroad," C. H. Parrish—Text, Acts 1:8; "The Bible and Africa," Rev. J. T. Brown.

And so the book contains quite a number of useful and helpful hints in our early missionary efforts, and we hope to revise it and put it in print again; In Our Stead, a little booklet or possibly 80 or 90 pages, is also out of print, and we cannot secure one for revision. We have always felt that with pictures we appeal to the eye, the most important window of the soul, and this is especially so to a people not too far removed from many traits of children, as in our group.

BAPTIST WASTE IS ATTACKED
BY DR. L. G. JORDAN
Veteran Historian in Analysis of Money Raised by Church; Asks Questions

Miami, Fla.—(Special)—Some very interesting questions were asked by Dr. L. G. Jordan, Nashville, Tennessee, veteran Baptist leader and historian for the National Baptist Convention, Inc., shortly before leaving the city Tuesday for the Bahamas Islands, where he will endeavor to form associations of the more than 16,000 Baptists in that area.

The noted historian-preacher urges that the national body appoint a special commission that will stop the existing waste in the organization. He feels that sufficient money is being raised by Negro Baptists to pay for their publishing plant and to run all of their schools if properly accounted for and spent honestly.

"We have forty-eight Baptist state conventions," Dr. Jordan pointed out in discussing the matter, "each of which will raise an average or $1,500, a total of $72,000 this year.

"Each of these state bodies has a Sunday school, a B.Y.P.U., and a Woman's Convention, or a total of three auxiliaries, making a grand total of 2,100 auxiliaries in the denomination. Each of these auxiliaries will raise an average of $100.00, or a total of $210,000.00 during the year.

"We have 800 district associations each of which will raise an average of $125.00, a total of $100,000.00.

"Furthermore, the 800 associations have three auxiliaries, each consisting of a Sunday school, B.Y.P.U., and a Woman's Convention, making a total of 2,200 auxiliaries. Each of these auxiliaries will raise an average of $80.00 each, or a total of $176,000.00!"

And then, in conclusion, Dr. Jordan asserts that the non-white Baptists of this country will raise, dur-

*ing "this year of our Lord, in the name of missions
and Christian education, at least $574,000.00.*

*Dr. Jordan has seen many years of service to his
church and is still actively engaged in its work. He
admits that his figures are very, very conservative.*

*"Where does the money go?" Dr. Jordan replies,
when asked as to what he thinks happens to this huge
sum of money, and adds further, "Why ask me?
How can I know?"*

—The Atlanta Daily World

In the eyes of men, I have injured myself when, on
many occasions, I have said, "When we are employed
to manage and look after any cause, and we grow fat
and rich while the cause grows lean and poor, there is
some stealing going on."

In one state, one of the most outstanding men ran
for the presidency of the Baptist State Convention and
was defeated by a former president. After that, he
never got the floor to speak, nor was he appointed to a
committee. I spoke to one of the leaders about it pri-
vately, and his reply was, "Brother, we know how to
eliminate them when they need it." This sort of un-
brotherly and un-Christian conduct among men calling
themselves teachers of righteousness will surely bring
them sorrow and may reach their children. See the
story of Joseph and his brethren.

CHAPTER XIII

There Are Things Of More Value Than Money

OME YEARS AGO A rabid politician of the South, in an effort to win votes made a vicious attack on the Negro as a whole and, as I now recall, among other things, said: "The nigger, in pursuit of a dollar, will crawl on his belly, and roll over in the dirt for money. He will kiss the hand that smites him or the boot that kicks him for money." It did seem harsh; but the speaker was seeking office and found to abuse a people who had done him no wrong and who had been robbed of their votes had no way to punish their traducers, and that such an appeal stirred up hate against us, and so like many others who used this method, he won. But today, as one listens in over the radio to the debasing way which some of the more learned of our group sing the religious folk songs, belittle the religion of their fathers, the uppishness with which they decry character and goodness, he cannot help remembering this tirade by the politician.

Now come the following, which as a sign for our love for money and applause is a real disgrace upon the whole group. It is an Editorial in the Opportunity.

—*Journal of Negro Life*

Anent the treatment of the Negro in literature and on the screen, it is interesting to note the reactions of the "untutored" African who has been depicted in a thousand travel books—unnumbered studies, countless school books—as an ignorant savage. Just now there is a popular motion picture being shown in the British Isles called *Sanders of the River*, by Edgar Wallace, an English novelist. In commenting on this picture and novel, Zik, whose column captioned "Inside Stuff," in a regular feature of the *African Morning Post*, a lively and well-edited daily of Accra, Gold Coast, West Africa, bitterly attacks the treatment of the Negro in literature and on the screen in the following language:

"Again, in the realm of literature, we find the black race portrayed as sub-human. In fact, most of the novels which have earned a great reputation have done so at the expense of the black races.

"Take the modern novels in America and England, for example; you will never find a novelist who will have the moral courage to give the black man or woman a position of respect in his characters. Blacks are either clowns, servants, or imbeciles, so far as their characterization is concerned...

"Outside of an all-Negro production, one hardly finds Hollywood or Elstree ready to portray the African man as a hero, or an African woman as a heroine."

But Zik reserves his most annihilating criticism for American Negro actors and actresses, especially Paul Robeson, admittedly one of the most popular and one of the most gifted of American artists. Discussing the picture Sanders of the River, he says:

"We are not interested in the portrayal of the African as a god or as a devil, necessarily, in this instance. What we are racking our brains over is the mentality of those people of African descent who, on the one hand, would criticize the attempts of Europeans to undervalue our culture, and, on the other hand, would bow down to the almighty pound, shilling, pence."

The acting of Mr. Robeson, and others, of the debasing traits of the African simply deepens, broadcasts, and strengthens the foolish ideas of African inferiority.

Now that Italy has decided to destroy Abyssinia, it is suspiciously suggestive that this play should be circumnavigating the world at this time. Now, for the intellectual flower of that race to act the part of African inferiority; for one of the most artistic of African descendants to lend his ability and rare talent to advertise and exploit the baseness and "inferiority" of his own race, is, to our idea, the height of race degeneration; it shows that, for money, the best talents of that race can be paid to decry, and add the notion of "racial inferiority" to the world. We are quite sure no Jew could be employed thus, to hire out his artistic ability; nor any other race. There is evidently a lack of something in the character of the man or woman who is thus employed.

Bahama Islands Bethel Baptist Church (The Colony's Oldest Local Institution—1801)

The following captures highlights of my 1935 visit to the Bahamas Islands. "Rev. L.G. Jordan, historian, and a member of the National Baptist Commission to the Island, preached in the Zion Baptist Church at 11 a.m. Sunday.

"The Doctor dwelt on the need and value of teaching, asserting that teaching occurs nearly as often in the Bible as preaching.

"He urged that Bahama Baptists be united so the National Baptist Convention may aid in pushing an extension of the American Baptist Theological Seminary in these Islands.

"'We come to help Bahama Baptists organize The Bahama Baptist Convention. It has been done, and now we go home and will report to the National Baptist Convention in New York, next September, of what has been done and your wish and promise. It may follow in October or November that a Preacher's Training School will open here,' said he.

"The Commission consists of Dr. A.M. Townsend;

Red. J.R. Evans, D.D.; Rev. L.G. Jordan, D.D.; Rev. S.A. Sampson; and Rev. R.L. Jones.

"The contemplated school, when plans for it are worked out, will be under the care of the Home, Foreign, and Sunday School Boards of the National Baptist Convention in the United States of America.

"At St. Paul, Sunday evening, Dr. Jordan stressed the opportunities of the islanders, urging that they learn to co-operate in observing the laws of God and our government.

"'The Negro of Jamaica was freed in 1833, of the Bahamas in 1838, those in the United States in 1865, but no group of us has been as helpful and interested in Africa. Our motherland, as we should have been, and I fear our selfishness has given us much trouble.

"'When a race's ways please the Lord, he maketh their enemies to be at peace with them,' he concluded.

"The final meeting of the Commission was held in Salem, after which the party sailed by the *S.S. Ena K.* for the U.S.A.

—*The Nassau Daily Tribune, May 27, 1935*

Was It Not a Baptist Machine?

Not many days ago, there was seen on a main highway a very strange and interesting-looking, yet mysterious machine. Beside it stood a very intelligent-looking attendant in whose care was this strange machine. So very odd was it, and so absorbed in it was the attendant, that the attention of the many travelers was soon called to the machine and its queer attendant.

A large crowd of interested travelers soon crowded around the machine and finally asked what sort of machine it was, and for what purpose it was made. After many such searching questions, the attendant finally said, "This machine manufactures oil."

Instantly the demand was made: "Let us see some of the oil that this machine makes."

But the attendant replied with seeming pride, "There is none of the oil of this machine on exhibition. It takes all the oil that it makes to oil itself and keep it in running shape."

With a hearty laugh, one of the oldest inquirers shouted, "It must be a Baptist machine, then, for Baptists are the only organized machine in existence that uses all of its products and oil to keep itself running."

Is there any other organized denominational machine that consumes all of its own output itself?

Buy a Bond

As a pioneer in the Negro Baptist program, I started the work for the reorganization of our Foreign Mission activities about three months after the death of Dr. L. M. Luke, who had held the position of secretary only one month before he passed to the Great Beyond. The National Baptist Convention itself had just been through the process of consolidation whereby the three styled national bodies were merged into one—its present form—at Atlanta, September 1895. Although the Foreign Mission work was the oldest of the Boards, it was facing a state of almost total collapse, so that on entering upon my new duties there was not a sheet of paper, not even a pencil on hand. It was necessary to begin at the very bottom. During that first day I succeeded in locating the Board's property—two or three chairs, a small "Jumbo" stove and an antiquated desk, which was entirely empty. No records, nothing to give even the slightest hint of previous efforts. Later on I learned that Mrs. Lucy Coles had a small book of records, and she gave it to me, but it furnished no information concerning the work. There was not a single missionary in the field; the whole enterprise was at the vanishing point. When the Board notified me that I had been elected to succeed Dr. Luke, they also informed me that there was $13.00 in the treasury, but they decided to spend this money to notify the Baptist brotherhood that I had been chosen to be Secretary of the Foreign Mission Board, so that it was up to me to cover as much territory as I could by traveling incessantly, speaking wherever I could get opportunity to create interest in the sorrows of Africa and our brethren across the seas. By the grace of God I did what I could until my physical breakdown—more than a quarter if a century later.

In September 1896, the publishing of Sunday school literature was launched by the National Baptist Convention, U.S.A., with Dr. R.H. Boyd as secretary. His book gives me credit for my part in making the venture a success.

Three years later, Dr. Isaac was called from Texas to organize our young people, and I helped him.

In September 1900, in Richmond, Virginia, our women's organization was formed, and the Foreign Mission Board had spent over $500.00 in preparing the way, and for five years gave desk space and clerical service free, to further the cause. As to our publishing house, at Chicago in September 1915, because of our over-confidence in the brethren we trusted, all was lost, and Baptists were forced to start all over again, and my part was to help plan our present Sunday School Publishing Board—now a million-dollar printing plant, the largest thing ever achieved by our group, the Morris Memorial Building, 4th Avenue at Cedar Street, Nashville, Tennessee. With "Buy a Bond" as their slogan, Negro Baptists are buying $600,000.00 worth of legal, gilt-edged bonds to free the National Baptist Convention from every debt against every one of its Boards, rightly looking on it as a form of stewardship to use its money as serving God and man with their earthly substance, although it is not a gift, for the bonds pay 5 percent! Look it up and "buy a bond."

CHAPTER XIV

A Shelter For The Aged

HERE WERE ONLY A handful of ordained preachers who came out of bondage in 1861. Historians say that there were not more than two
dozen independent Baptist churches among Negroes at
the close of the Civil War. For 250 years the ministers
who preached to our group pastored both master and
slave, the one in the main auditorium, the other in the
gallery specially provided for them.

Today there are 21,000 Negro Baptist ministers,
hundreds of the older ones are being forced out of service and being replaced by the younger and better prepared preachers. These unfortunates, now above
sixty-five, were giants in their day; though imperfect
in themselves they preached a perfect gospel, thereby
saving the race from infidelity during the past seventy
years, and making the group strong against the on-
slaughts of Bolshevism and the forces which seek to

overthrow Christianity and orderly governments.

Our white brethren, North and South, maintain homes for aged ministers and are well able to do so, because of their superior advantages and salaries, but so far as we know the aged Negro minister is barred.

Recently the National Baptist Convention through the American Baptist Home Mission Society secured the former site of the Roger Williams University in Nashville, and plans are being laid to use it as a refuge for aged ministers and Christian workers.

Dr. J. B. Lawrence, Secretary-Treasurer of the Home Mission Board of the Southern Baptist Convention, expresses the sentiment which should be echoed, not only by our white Baptist brethren, but by God's children everywhere.

"The Negroes should not be overlooked. There are 10,000,000 of them in the South. The leadership of the Negro race lies largely with its ministry. We should never forget that the foundations of many of our fortunes were laid by slave labor."

This little help asked for the old gospel warriors who led and taught the children of a group and who served others without pay, for 250 years, is reasonable indeed. "This obligation therefore is laid upon all of our Father's children."

The Enemy of All the People

Just as long as things go on as the following , and I am able to get around, I am ready to fight the liquor traffic, because of the injury it does my people, yes, and all the people.

> *"I will not quarrel with you about opinions. See that your heart is right towards God, that you know and love the Lord Jesus Christ, that you love your neighbor and walk as your Master walked, and I desire no more."*
>
> —John Wesley

The *Chicago Herald and Examiner* of March 6, 1934, says: "Shocking evidence of how Chicago's high school girls and boys—children ranging between 13 and 16 years of age—are being lured into depravity by saloon keepers who flagrantly violate the law. . . Drunkenness and laxity of morals are common in the dimly lit back rooms of these saloons, many of which carry on their vicious trade in the very shadows of the city's schools.

"Sprawled on the floor and asleep at the long tables were a dozen young boys and nearly as many girls. Some were obviously 14 and 15 years old. The older ones were 17 and 18. These children were students of Lake View High School. . . A score or more couples were locked in tight embrace. Others staggered about the dance floor.

"'The high school kids make up 90% of our parties,' stated a Lake View senior. A member of the committee pointed to ten kegs of beer—all they have for a party of schoolchildren. . . Girls have 'passed out,' their heads on their escorts' laps. Boys have fallen asleep on the shoulders of their dates. . . This is how 'temperance' is being promoted in Chicago under repeal. The saloon keepers, brewers, and distillers are making the profits, but the children 'pay the freight.'"

Drunken Driving

Since repeal the increase in driving-while-drunk in typical cities, as reported to the International Association of Chiefs of Police, on December 26, 1934, is as follows: Los Angeles, 479 percent; Cincinnati, 380 percent; Philadelphia, 300 percent; New Orleans, 122 percent.

The *Chicago Tribune*, a wet paper, on July 18, 1934, editorially said that automobile fatalities chargeable to drunken driving had increased, since repeal, fourfold.

Traffic accidents caused by liquor in Detroit increased 164 percent after repeal, as reported in Official Traffic Police Survey. Drunken drivers increased 162 per cent after repeal in Philadelphia, as reported by the Assistant Superintendent of Police.

4 Killed Each Hour In '34 Auto Crashes

Hartford, Connecticut, December 27 (UP)—Every 15 minutes during the past year someone was killed in an automobile accident; and every 31 seconds someone was injured. These figures, compiled by insurance statisticians, show a total of more than 36,000 deaths and more than 1,000,000 injured in more than 900,000 automobile accidents. The fatality toil was an increase of

16 percent over figures for 1933, and a slight decrease in frequency of accidents.

Thank God For Friends

> "To God's chariots two celestial charges are yoked: Omniscience and Omnipotence; the rim of those chariot wheels is so high that it is dreadful, and full of eyes before and behind. To set oneself against God's purpose is to be trampled to pieces under the feet of those steeds, and ground to powder beneath those wheels; but it is no less certain that to work for and with God is to be borne along irresistibly toward the goal of consummate victory and final glory!"
> —Arthur T. Pierson

> "Unless our souls had root in soil divine
> We could not bear earth's overwhelming strife
> The fiercest pain that racks this heart of mine
> Convinces me of everlasting life."

I am debtor both to the dead whom I knew in life, and to the many living whom I know, for whatever good has come to others out of my poor imperfect life. During the 63 years I have served as one of God's messengers to a sinful world, I have been very active, and am yet active, and I am sure I have grown more unselfish with the years.

At times my denominational ideals have annoyed some who profess to be liberal—they presuming too much on the goodness of God and too little on the justice of God, and that too in the face of the Bible in which both are promised. But my brethren, everywhere, have been most patient with me and kind to the point of indulgence.

To know the results of my long life, see the six church-houses built, the many hundreds baptized the four trips to Africa, the four to the islands of the Sea, the one to South America, the eight trips to Europe; then see my nearly 100 African foster children brought to the States and trained: and lastly, the army of preachers, many now in middle life, who say that my enthusiasm, earnestness and illustrative story-telling— all have been inspiration to them. Through these services of the past and what I can do on to the end, I hope to live on and on.

I feel doubly grateful to all who in any way helped my work as pastor, Foreign Mission Secretary, and historian, and now as an associate with our Foreign Mission Secretary. It is my earnest prayer that our Secretary, Dr. J.H. Jackson, is God's "ram in the Thicket." We have found in him a man who has youth, education, and a fine personality and withal a good preacher. Under his leadership may every agency be yoked up in a great effort for Africa's redemption—the greatest ever known. I shall not only do my bit, but my very best by prayer, voice and pen.

Yours in his service,

L.G. Jordan
Historian of the National Baptist
Convention; Associate Secretary
Foreign Mission Board

Mrs. Susie A. Jordan

Mrs. Susie Allston Jordan began a career which has been both useful and varied by being the first Colored girl to pass through the public schools of Haverhill, Massachusetts, she graduated with honors from Haverhill High School. She followed up her training studying in Boston and New York; Mrs. Jordan had the privilege of education in the universities of each of the two cities above mentioned. She was a teacher of Household Economics, graduating from Boston School of Domestic Science. Mrs. Jordan has rare literary gifts and served for several years as secretary to Rev. L.K. Williams, D.D., President of the National Baptist Convention. She is editor of the *Sunday School Informer*; the quality of her work takes high rank among the best productions of present-day religious teachers. Mrs. Jordan is now in the employ of the Sunday School Publishing Board as secretary to Dr. S.N. Vass, Secretary of Religious Education. Her special interest lies in the field of Daily Vacation Bible School promotion, and in this line she merits the statement made by the head of her department in Hampton Institute while she was an instructor in that famous Institution:

"She is a born executive."

Their knowledge of, interest in, and love for all the people made them believe and so they spoke.

"The message of God to the world is the everlasting gospel. It is no new upstart doctrine—an after thought

of God. It is as old as eternity, yet as new as the last sun's rays that kiss the morning flower."
—Z.D. Lewis, D. D., Pastor Second Baptist Church, Richmond, Va., July, 1896.

"Indeed, L.M. Luke was a high type of pure Christian manhood; too broad to be jealous or envious, too noble to be suspicious or peevish, and too intelligent to be either cowardly, compromising, arrogant or egotistic, relying upon truth and the justice of his cause for winning."
—C. H.Payne, D. D., Consul to St. Thomas and the Virgin Islands, July 1896

"No grander subject could engage our minds than the salvation of millions in Africa who are dying for the bread of life. We have met to think, talk, pray and give in order that the gospel may be given to Africa, the land of our fathers."
—E. K. Love, *National Baptist Magazine*, July 1896

"I do not overlook the value of religion and culture, for they are as valuable for the Negro as for any race; but it is a pretty hard thing to give a man much culture when he has no house to live in, and it is equally hard to make a good Christian of a hungry man."
—Booker T. Washington, President of Tuskegee, *National Baptist Magazine*

"In our own march, amid the many persecutions

heaped upon the race, I urge that you exercise great patience and then exhort your people to patience. Many of us expect far too much of the race in this day. Our demands are entirely too great. We are asking for fifty thousand first-class school teachers; twenty-five thousand pulpits are demanding educated and trained preachers; doctors, lawyers, statesmen, and men of all classes of professions are demanded for the race, and only one generation has passed since the shackles fell from our limbs. The time we have been free is too short to have developed all these and at the same time accumulate from nothing a billion dollars' worth of property. My friends, I urge you to be encouraged. We have done well. The next generation will do far better.

—E.C. Morris

Glossary

African American Registry—See African American Registry – www.aaregistry.org.

Anent—Old English *on emn, on efn*, on even ground with.

Brush Arbor—The Brush Arbor meeting got its name from the crude structure under which these meetings took place. Brush arbors were roughed-in shelters made deep in the forest they of upright poles driven into the ground; long poles were laid across the top and tied together in lattice fashion to serve as a support for a primitive roof of brush and hay that served to protect the worshiper and slaves from the elements.

B.Y.P.U.—Baptist Young People Union. It is absolutely essential that the church have constantly in training a group of devoted young men and women who will, on the morrow, assume the role of leadership in the various departments of church life. The B.Y.P.U., the recognized training service of the church, meets this need.

Cocklebur Tea—In the early days of the Cherokee, cocklebur were considered to have unusual powers. The cocklebur plant is coarse and thorny. When the bur was prepared, it was used as an herbal remedy; the seed oil is edible by humans.

Devil and Tom Walker—He is considered the man who gave his soul to the devil in exchange for wealth.

Emancipation Proclamation—President Abraham Lincoln issued the Emancipation Proclamation on January 1, 1863, as the nation approached its third year of bloody civil war. The proclamation declared that "all persons held as slaves within the rebellious states are and henceforward shall be free."

Foreign Mission Board—Rev. W.W. Colley of Virginia, who served as a missionary in Africa under the Foreign Mission Board of the Southern Baptist Convention, returned to the states in 1879 imbued with the desire to awaken colored Baptists to a greater love for God and Africa. He interested the most thoughtful among pastors; after months of travel and personally touching hundreds of them, the call was sent forth, summoning for the first time Negro Baptists to a well thought-out national meeting. The Convention began with a Foreign Mission Board, a Home Mission Board, and an Educational Board. The Foreign Mission Board of

Philadelphia, Pennsylvania, sent its first company of missionaries, consisting of six persons, to West Africa in 1883.

George Lisle—1783. Rev George Lisle, Rev. Moses Baker, and Rev. George Givens, emancipated Negroes and Baptist preachers, left America as volunteer missionaries to the West Indies.

Hardtack—This was the most famous American Civil War staple food. Hard as a rock, hardtack crackers fed hungry Union soldiers throughout the war. For slaves, it was what they earned: Hardtack and navy beans made up their "salary."

Indigo Mud—Indigo is a plant. Studies indicate alcohol extract from the leaves and stems protect the liver and ward off certain kinds of chemical damage.

Kith—Friends; acquaintances

Kith and Kin—Old English, friends and relatives

Liberia—Africa's first republic was founded in 1822 as a result of the efforts to the American Colonization Society to settle freed slaves in West Africa. The society functioned over the course of 40 years; about 12,000 slaves were voluntarily

relocated. Monrovia, the capital city of the
West African nation, was named in honor of
U.S. President James Monroe, a prominent sup-
porter of the colonization of Liberia, along with
Washington, D.C. as the U.S. capitol. Strange
to say, the very first practical step toward the
solution of the problem of the black man was
taken by a black man, Paul Cuffe. In 1815, one
year before the organization of the Colonization
Society, he carried to Africa at his own expense
a score of his countrymen, whom he landed at
Sierra Leone. This feat strengthened the faith
of the Society in the colonization idea. (See
L.G.Jordan, *Pebbles from an African Beach* and *Up
the Ladder in Mission.*)

Mound Bayou—Isaiah Montgomery was born into
slavery at Davis Bend, the plantation of Joseph
Davis, the brother Jefferson Davis, the president of the Southern Confederacy. His father,
Benjamin, managed the plantation for Davis
until the end of the Civil War and was able to
purchase it after the end of hostilities. He estab-
lished a prosperous colony of fellow freedmen
for several years, but agricultural prices fell and
severe winter flooding ruined their levees.
When his loan fell overdue, the property was
sold back to the Davis family. Ben Montgomery died in 1877, but his dream of establish-
ing an independent black colony was taken up

by his son Isaiah, who later founded the settlement of Mound Bayou. When the colonists, many of whom had been slaves in Mississippi, complained about the rigorous conditions, Montgomery challenged them: "You have for centuries hewed down forests at the request of the master. Could you not do it for yourselves and your children into successive generations, that they may worship and develop under your own vine and fig tree?" (See *The Rise and fall of Jim Crow*, PBS.)

Peck of Meal—Field slaves lived mostly on a diet of cornmeal, salt herring, and pork. They had two meals a day: a breakfast at twelve noon, and a dinner much later. Solom Northrup, a slave from a Louisiana plantation said, when describing his meals given to him by the planter, "All that is allowed them is corn and bacon, which is given out in the corn-crib and smoke-house every Sunday morning. Each one receives, as his weekly allowance, three and a half pounds of bacon, and corn enough to make a peck of meal. (See Oracle and thinkquest at www.thinkquest.org.)

Providence—God, especially when conceived as omnisciently directing the Universe and the affairs of humankind with wise benevolence. A manifestation of divine care or direction.

Fannie Jordan, Lewis Garnett Jordan's daughter and my grandmother

From left, my mother Elleary Doris Williams Smith, and my aunts
Emma Sykes Harrison and Cynthia Sykes Butler

*First row, from left, Robin Renee Cooper, Emma Sykes
Harrison, Cynthia Sykes Butler; second row, Adelaide
Sykes Langley and Elleary Doris Williams Smith*

*From left, my daughter Robin, me, and Darlene Butler
Davis, Lewis Garnett Jordan's great-granddaughters*

My mother, Elleary Doris Williams Smith

My daughter, Robin Renee Cooper, and my son, Daniel Louis Cooper, at the Schomburg. It was the first time we had the original edition of On Two Hemispheres *in our hands.*

*A dream come true—my first public admission, to Alex Haley,
that I wanted to become a writer.*

My uncle Chandler Whitmore Sykes, grandson of L.G. Jordan

From right, Cynthia Butler Sykes, and Rhea Davis, her granddaugh-
ter, Lewis Garnett's great-great-granddaughter

CPSIA information can be obtained at www.ICGtesting.com
Printed in the USA
BVOW07s2314260813

329501BV00002B/13/P